JOURNAL OF APPLIE

C000049931

VOLUME 6, NUMBER 3, 2003

SPECIAL ISSUE:
Training Nonhuman Primates Using Positive Reinforcement Techniques

GUEST EDITORS:
Mark J. Prescott and Hannah M. Buchanan-Smith

JOURNAL OF APPLIED ANIMAL WELFARE SCIENCE, 6(3), 157–161
Copyright © 2003, Lawrence Erlbaum Associates, Inc.

GUEST EDITORS' INTRODUCTION

Training Nonhuman Primates Using Positive Reinforcement Techniques

Mark J. Prescott

Research Animals Department
Royal Society for the Prevention of Cruelty to Animals
West Sussex, England

Hannah M. Buchanan-Smith

Department of Psychology
University of Stirling

Training nonhuman primates to cooperate with routine scientific, husbandry, and veterinary procedures is recommended as good practice by many legislative and professional guidelines (Home Office, 1989; International Primatological Society, 1989). Despite this, the scientific literature on this topic is sparse and disparate, and training is not used as widely as it might be. This may be due to the paucity of information on how to train and its potential benefits, together with the lack of reliable assessment of the potential costs of training. Whatever the reason, it is unfortunate because training can reduce the fear, anxiety, and distress known to be caused to primates by many traditional methods of carrying out procedures (Reinhardt, Liss, & Stevens, 1995).

Primates in the laboratory may experience a plethora of potential stressors including physical and chemical restraint, venipuncture, injection, and participation in other husbandry routines such as catching, cage change, and weighing. Training them to cooperate voluntarily, using positive reinforcement training (PRT) techniques, is one means of significantly reducing the adverse impact of such procedures and husbandry routines on them and, therefore, is a refinement. Refinement

Requests for reprints should be sent to Mark J. Prescott, Research Animals Department, RSPCA, Horsham, West Sussex, RH13 9RS, England. E-mail: mprescott@rspca.org.uk

is vitally important for humanitarian reasons and for satisfying broad legal principles. Furthermore, techniques that reduce or eliminate adverse effects not only benefit animal welfare (Bassett, Buchanan-Smith, McKinley, & Smith, 2003/this issue) but also can enhance the quality of scientific research because suffering in animals can result in physiological changes that are, at least, likely to increase variability in experimental data and, at worst, may invalidate the research (Reinhardt, 2003/this issue). Techniques that reduce sources of variability also have the potential of reducing the number of animals required in a given protocol (Brockway, Hassler, & Hicks, 1993).

Aside from reducing the stress associated with scientific procedures, PRT can be integrated into animal management practices to enhance the care and well-being of primates in captivity (Laule, Bloomsmith, & Schapiro, 2003/this issue). Examples of ways of doing this include reducing aggression and improving socialization (Schapiro, Bloomsmith, & Laule, 2003/this issue), reducing or eliminating abnormal behavior (Laule, 1993), or facilitating health inspection such as transponder reading, inspection of body parts, and weighing (Savastano, Hanson, & McCann, 2003/this issue). Therefore, PRT is a useful tool for the zoo as well as the laboratory (Colahan, & Breder, 2003/this issue; Savastano et al., 2003/this issue). In fact, PRT would be of no value to primates (or to those managing them) in relatively few captive situations.

In recognition of this, we coorganized a symposium at the Nineteenth Congress of the International Primatological Society, August 4 through 9, 2002, Beijing, China, to bring together individuals involved in primate training in zoos and in laboratories to discuss and share training information in an international forum (Prescott & Buchanan-Smith, 2002). We felt it timely to consider what use is currently made of PRT to train primates and how it can be used in the future. In particular, we encouraged contributors to provide quantitative data on the costs and benefits of PRT and/or clear practical guidance on its application. We are delighted to be able to publish the symposium papers, together with additional contributions, in this special issue of *Journal of Applied Animal Welfare Science.*

All the articles illustrate benefits to animals from PRT and, depending on the setting, to scientists, animal care staff, veterinarians, and, in the case of zoos, the visiting public. Some contributors go so far as to provide empirical data for assessing its effectiveness and value (McKinley, Buchanan-Smith, Bassett, & Morris, 2003/this issue; Schapiro et al., 2003/this issue). Significant refinements are described; sometimes for already refined procedures. Laule et al. (2003/this issue) give a protocol for cooperation with blood collection that does not feature the cage squeeze-back mechanism utilized in Reinhardt's (2003/this issue) protocol for this procedure. Scott, Pearce, Fairhall, Muggleton, and Smith (2003/this issue) describe training for leaving and returning to the homecage that has replaced use of the pole and collar system for this purpose in their laboratory. McKinley et al. (2003/this issue) describe a method for in homecage collection of urine (as a less-stressful alternative to blood sampling) that is a refinement of that of Anzenberger and Gossweiler (1993); however, as noted by the authors, collection of saliva may be a more satisfactory replacement for blood (and urine) sampling.

One important theme in all the articles is that training is a joint venture between human and nonhuman primate and can lead to a closer, richer relationship between the two. Quite apart from the benefits that accrue from training specific behaviors, the training process can, through simple habituation, enhance the well-being of captive nonhuman primates and lead to positive changes in the attitude to animals of the staff involved (Bayne, 2002).

The principal cost of training is the initial time investment, but this generally is small and often is recouped within a short period. Furthermore, it is more than outweighed by the benefits in terms of animal welfare, facilitated management, and reduction in the variability of research data (McKinley et al., 2003/this issue; Reinhardt, 2003/this issue; Savastano et al., 2003/this issue; Schapiro et al., 2003/this issue). The most efficient training is likely to take advantage of the animal's natural behavioral repertoire (McKinley et al., 2003/this issue). There may be other costs aside from time investment; there is a possibility that reinforcing animals for urinating on command could lead to urinary tract infection. Therefore, it is important to think carefully about the possible consequences of training before embarking on any training program and, if in any doubt, to consult a training specialist. Otherwise, one could, for example, inadvertently reinforce the wrong behavior or produce unwanted changes in behavior outside of training.

Although primates can be trained for cooperation with a wide variety of tasks, all primates necessarily cannot be trained for the same task. This may be because of the aptitudes of different species (Savastano et al., 2003/this issue), sexes and individuals (Schapiro et al., 2003/this issue), and ages. Some characteristics of the species, such as social hierarchy, also may affect what can be achieved. They may limit learning or performance of a trained behavior within the context of the social group (Schapiro et al., 2003/this issue). However, it should be noted that individual primates often are more relaxed when in groups than when isolated and can learn socially through observation of their conspecifics and congeners (Prescott & Buchanan-Smith, 1999). This ability can be utilized by the trainer: Allowing animals to be observers during training sessions may enable them to be trained more rapidly because of their familiarity with the training situation (Savastano et al.,2003/this issue).

The advantages and disadvantages of PRT techniques as applied to primates in the laboratory deserve more extensive exploration—both for the sake of the primates involved and the quality of scientific data obtained. Primates can be trained to perform tests of cognitive ability to generate data for use in biomedical research. In such cases, what matters to the animal is not our motives for the training but the impact of training on the welfare of the animal. It is often claimed that such training is an enriching experience for the animals involved, but there are little data available to substantiate this claim. If such training is enriching, what are the consequences—in terms of animal welfare—of stopping the test when the experiment or study ends? In either case, we concur with the view of Scott et al. (2003/this issue) that training must be seen as an adjunct to the provision of adequate socialization with conspecifics in high quality diverse housing systems and not as an alternative to such provision.

In investigating, implementing, and discussing primate training, it has been possible for us to identify many other questions. What are the best and most humane training techniques for the species and/or tasks? What is the optimal length of training session for particular species, tasks and group sizes? What are the effects of training animals on zoo visitor viewing behavior and perceptions? Obviously, there is a need for further research and for sharing of information through publication of empirical findings concerning both successful and unsuccessful training attempts. However, unanswered questions should not be used as excuses for avoiding the implementation of proven, safe, and effective refinements involving PRT.

In summary, we believe that, as a general principle, thorough consideration always should be given to the use of training as a refinement to traditional methods of carrying out procedures and that reward should be used as a reinforcer (positive reinforcement). Negative reinforcement should be used only when positive alternatives have been exhausted. We hope that this special issue will encourage further and wider application of PRT to primate management, care, and use and will aid laboratory animal care staff, scientists, research students, veterinarians, and zoo keepers in applying PRT safely and effectively.

ACKNOWLEDGMENTS

During the writing of this article, and editing of this special issue, Hannah M. Buchanan-Smith was supported by a grant from the European Union (QLRT–2001–00028). We gratefully acknowledge the informative and thought-provoking discussions we have shared with all those involved with training primates and, in particular, Vicky Melphi, Tessa Smith, Leah Scott, Peter Pearce, Josie Harder, Jean McKinley, and Verity Bowell. Special thanks to Kenneth Shapiro for the opportunity to edit this special issue and for all of his assistance. The Royal Society for the Prevention of Cruelty to Animals is opposed to all experiments or procedures that case pain, suffering, or distress, and works to promote initiatives that lead to greater application of the Three Rs—replacing animals with humane alternatives, reducing the number of animals used, and refining husbandry and procedures to reduce suffering and improve animal welfare.

REFERENCES

Anzenberger, G., & Gossweiler, H. (1993). How to obtain individual urine samples from undisturbed marmoset families. *American Journal of Primatology, 31,* 223–230.

Bassett, L., Buchanan-Smith, H. M., McKinley, J., & Smith, T. E. (2003/this issue). Effects of training on stress-related behavior of the common marmoset (*Callithrix jacchus*) in relation to coping with routine husbandry procedures. *Journal of Applied Animal Welfare Science, 6,* 221–233.

Bayne, K. (2002). Development of the human–research animal bond and its impact on animal well-being. *Institute for Laboratory Animal Research, 43,* 4–9.

Brockway, B. P., Hassler, C. R., & Hicks, N. (1993). Minimizing stress during physiological monitoring. In S. M. Niemi & J. E. Willson (Eds.), *Refinement and reduction in animal testing* (pp. 56–69). Bethesda, MD: Scientists Center for Animal Welfare.

Colahan, H., & Breder, C. (2003/this issue). Primate training at Disney's Animal Kingdom. *Journal of Applied Animal Welfare Science, 6,* 235–246.

Home Office. (1989). *Code of practice for the housing and care of animals used in scientific procedures.* London: Her Majesty's Stationery Office.

International Primatological Society. (1989). IPS International guidelines for the acquisition, care and breeding of nonhuman primates. *Primate Report, 25,* 3–27.

Laule, G. (1993). The use of behavioral management techniques to reduce or eliminate abnormal behavior. *Animal Welfare Information Center Newsletter, 4,* 1–2, 8–11.

Laule, G. E., Bloomsmith, M. A., & Schapiro, S. J. (2003/this issue). The use of positive reinforcement training techniques to enhance the care, management, and welfare of laboratory primates. *Journal of Applied Animal Welfare Science, 6,* 163–173.

McKinley, J., Buchanan-Smith, H. M., Bassett, L., & Morris K. (2003/this issue). Training common marmosets (*Callithrix jacchus*) to cooperate during routine laboratory procedures: Ease of training and time investment. *Journal of Applied Animal Welfare Science, 6,* 209–220.

Prescott, M. J., & Buchanan-Smith, H. M. (1999). Intra- and inter-specific social learning of a novel food task in two species of tamarin. *International Journal of Comparative Psychology, 12,* 71–92.

Prescott, M. J., & Buchanan-Smith, H. M. (2002). Training primates. In *Caring for primates: Abstracts of the 19th Congress of the International Primatological Society* (p. 180). Beijing: Mammalogical Society of China.

Reinhardt, V. (2003/this issue). Working with rather than against macaques during blood collection. *Journal of Applied Animal Welfare Science, 6,* 189–197.

Reinhardt, V., Liss, C., & Stevens, C. (1995). Restraint methods of laboratory nonhuman primates: A critical review. *Animal Welfare, 4,* 221–238.

Savastano, G., Hanson, A., & McCann, C. (2003/this issue). The development of an operant conditioning training program for New World primates at the Bronx Zoo. *Journal of Applied Animal Welfare Science, 6,* 247–261.

Schapiro, S. J., Bloomsmith, M. A., & Laule, G. E. (2003/this issue). Positive reinforcement training as a technique to alter nonhuman primate behavior: Quantitative assessments of effectiveness. *Journal of Applied Animal Welfare Science, 6,* 175–189.

Scott, L., Pearce, P., Fairhall, S., Muggleton, N., & Smith, J. (2003/this issue). Training nonhuman primates to cooperate with scientific procedures in applied biomedical research. *Journal of Applied Animal Welfare Science, 6,* 199–207.

JOURNAL OF APPLIED ANIMAL WELFARE SCIENCE, 6(3), 163–173
Copyright © 2003, Lawrence Erlbaum Associates, Inc.

The Use of Positive Reinforcement Training Techniques to Enhance the Care, Management, and Welfare of Primates in the Laboratory

Gail E. Laule

Active Environments
Lompoc, California

Mollie A. Bloomsmith

TECHLab
Zoo Atlanta, and
Yerkes National Primate Research Center
Atlanta, Georgia

Steven J. Schapiro

Department of Veterinary Sciences
The University of Texas M. D. Anderson Cancer Center

Handled frequently and subjected to a wide range of medical procedures that may be particularly invasive, nonhuman animals in a laboratory setting have unique needs. To produce the most reliable research results and to protect and enhance the well-being of the animals, it is desirable to perform these procedures with as little stress for the animals as possible. Positive reinforcement training can use targeted activities and procedures to achieve the voluntary cooperation of nonhuman primates. The benefits of such work include diminished stress on the animals, enhanced flexibility and reliability in data collection, and a reduction in the use of anesthesia. Training also provides the means to mitigate social problems, aid in introductions, reduce abnormal behavior, enhance enrichment programs, and increase the safety of at-

---

Request for reprints should be sent to Gail Laule, Active Environments, 7651 Santos Road, Lompoc, CA 93436. E-mail: moonshadowe@compuserve.com

tending personnel. This article describes the application of operant conditioning techniques to animal management.

The care and management of nonhuman animals in laboratories and zoos has evolved dramatically in the last 15 years. In the United States, the major impetus for change was the Animal Welfare Act (1987), which mandated that the psychological well-being of nonhuman primates and dogs be adequately addressed. By singling out these two specific groups of animals, the spotlight focused initially on the biomedical community, which was the first community to take action. They tackled the daunting task of determining what "psychological well-being" meant because nowhere was it clearly defined. This effort produced a thoughtful exploration of current animal care and management practices that was incredibly productive and much needed. Over the years, valuable information resulted from this process, including a number of excellent publications for example: Segal, 1989; Novak and Petto, 1991; Norton, Hutchins, Stevens, and Maple, 1995; and Shepherdson, Mellen, and Hutchins, 1998.

During this time, interest and support for the idea of using positive reinforcement training (PRT) to enhance the care and welfare of captive animals was also growing. The marine mammal community had been using PRT for many years to train dolphins and sea lions to do all those entertaining "tricks" the public loved to see. This community was also the first to recognize that those same techniques could be used to improve the care and welfare of these animals by gaining their voluntary cooperation in husbandry and veterinary procedures. It was through the handling of two performing male sea lions that the first author discovered a technique for reducing aggression and enhancing positive social interaction that is referred to as *cooperative feeding* (Laule & Desmond, 1991). In time, a PRT approach to captive animal management spread in many different contexts to the zoological and biomedical communities and, subsequently, to a vast array of species. Today, PRT is recognized more and more as an essential tool for the humane and effective management of captive animals. Now, too, greater effort is being placed on measuring the effects of training and the effectiveness of specific training techniques (McKinley, Buchanan-Smith, Bassett, & Morris, 2003/this issue; Schapiro, Bloomsmith & Laule, 2003/this issue). Addressing the needs of laboratory animals while meeting research objectives and implementing protocols should be the goal of every biomedical facility.

In this article we describe the application of operant conditioning techniques to a real-world animal management situation. Although we recognize that objective, operationally-defined terminology is an important part of the scientific endeavors of behavior analysts, we choose to use more casual language in this article. We believe that this style will be of more value to those who might apply the techniques to the nonhuman primates for whom they care.

OPERANT CONDITIONING

When we consider the impact of training on animal care and welfare, it is important to remember just what training is. *Training* is teaching. We teach animals to make a movement, to hold a position, or to tolerate a particular stimulus. To be an effective teacher or trainer requires the following attitudes and skills: (a) a high degree of patience, (b) empathy with your subject, (c) a cooperative relationship, (d) the ability to teach pieces that add up to the whole, and (e) the flexibility to adjust to what your subject "gives" you. Teaching and training require a willing subject who participates in the process, not a passive recipient of actions that are outside the subject's control.

It also is important to choose your training approach carefully. The fundamental principle of operant conditioning is that behavior is determined by its consequences. Behavior does not occur as isolated and unrelated events; the consequences that follow the actions of an animal, be they good, bad, or indifferent, will have an effect on the frequency with which those actions are repeated in the future. Operant conditioning offers two basic options for managing behavior: positive reinforcement and negative reinforcement or escape/avoidance. Both increase the chance that a behavior will occur. In a positive reinforcement-based system, animals are rewarded with something they like for responding appropriately to the caregiver's cues or commands. Operationally, we are gaining the animal's voluntary cooperation in the process. This differs from negative reinforcement training in which the animal performs the correct behavior to escape or avoid something unpleasant or aversive.

In the real world, it may not be feasible to utilize positive reinforcement exclusively. Our working principle is that the positive alternatives should be exhausted before any kind of negative reinforcement is employed. On the rare occasions when an escape-avoidance technique is necessary, its use should be kept to a minimum and balanced by using positive reinforcement the majority of the time.

Negative Reinforcement Training

Unfortunately, laboratory animal management practices traditionally have included a large measure of training through negative reinforcement. Although these techniques "get the job done," it could be argued that there is an inherent cost to the animal's overall welfare to be forced to cooperate through the threat of a negative event or experience that elicits fear or anxiety (Reinhardt, 1992).

Consider the animal who must receive an injection for a research protocol. Without training, the animal has no choice in how that event occurs. If negative reinforcement or escape/avoidance training is used, offering a choice—present a leg for the injection—requires the threat of an even more negative stimulus (a net or squeeze-cage back panel moving), thus exposing the animal to distress from both stimuli. Using a PRT approach, the animal is trained through shaping and rewards to present a leg voluntarily for an injection and concurrently desensitized to the procedure to reduce the associated fear or anxiety. When the injection is needed, it would seem logical to argue that having a clearer choice in how that event happens, and being less fearful of it, contributes to that animal's psychological well-being.

PRT

PRT techniques can provide the means to address a wide range of behavioral issues with primates in the laboratory. Training provides the tools to improve husbandry and veterinary care (Desmond & Laule, 1994; Reichard, Shellabarger, & Laule, 1992; Reinhardt, 1997; Stone, Laule, Bloomsmith, & Alford, 1995); reduce abnormal and/or stereotypic behavior (Laule, 1993); reduce aggression (Bloomsmith, Laule, Thurston, & Alford, 1994); improve socialization (Desmond, Laule, & McNary, 1987; Schapiro, Perlman, & Boudreau, 2001); enhance enrichment programs (Kobert, 1997; Laule & Desmond, 1998); and increase the safety of the attending personnel (Bloomsmith, 1992; Reinhardt, 1997). It also may improve the relationship between people and the animals in their care (Bayne, Dexter, & Strange, 1993; Bloomsmith, Lambeth, Stone, & Laule, 1997).

Training laboratory primates to cooperate voluntarily in husbandry, veterinary, and research procedures seems to have significant benefits for the animals. Animals are desensitized to frightening or painful events, such as receiving an injection; so the events become less frightening and less stressful (Moseley & Davis, 1989; Reinhardt, Cowley, Scheffler, Vertein, & Wegner, 1990). Voluntary cooperation reduces the need for physical restraint and/or anesthesia and, thus, the accompanying risks associated with those events (Bloomsmith, 1992; Reinhardt, Liss, & Stevens, 1995). Training can enhance animal welfare by providing animals the opportunity to work for food (Neuringer, 1969); achieve greater choice and control over daily events (Mineka, Gunnar, & Champoux, 1986); experience greater mental stimulation (Laule & Desmond, 1992); and experience other enriching results such as reduced self-directed behaviors, increased activity, and enhanced social interactions (Bloomsmith, 1992; Desmond et al., 1987; Laule, 1993). All these factors have been associated with enhanced psychological well-being (Hanson, Larson, & Snowdon, 1976; Markowitz, 1982).

Experience has shown that animals trained with positive reinforcement maintain a high degree of reliability in participating in husbandry and veterinary procedures and are less stressed while doing so (Reinhardt et al., 1990; Turkkan, Ator, Brady, & Craven, 1990). Investigators report evidence of these results in a variety of primate species including reductions in cortisol levels, stress-related abortions, physical resistance to handling, and fear responses such as fear-grinning, scream-ing, and acute diarrhea (Moseley & Davis, 1989; Reinhardt et al., 1990). Finally, many husbandry and veterinary procedures can be implemented with minimized disruption to all animals because the need to separate animals from their social groups for these procedures is reduced (Bloomsmith, 1992).

PRT Techniques

The following are a selection of training techniques that are valuable in a variety of management situations for nonhuman primates in a biomedical setting.

Conditioned reinforcer (bridge).   This is an initially meaningless signal that over time, when repeatedly paired with a primary reinforcer (i.e., food), be-comes a reinforcer. The most appropriate conditioned reinforcer in the laboratory setting is a hand-held clicker or a verbal "good." The conditioned reinforcer offers the trainer a way to communicate precisely to the animal the exact moment a de-sired behavioral response occurs. It's a way of saying, "Yes, that's exactly what I want," which is valuable information for the animal and can enhance learning.

Target.   A *target* is an object the animal is trained to touch. Targets can be made of various objects: a dowel or stick, plastic bottle, or a clip that can attach to the caging material. The target is a point of reference toward which the animal moves and is useful in several ways. First, the caregiver can control gross move-ment by rewarding the primate for moving toward the target when it is presented or for going to a target preplaced elsewhere in the cage. Second, the animal can be trained to stay at the target for a period. Socially housed primates can be trained to remain at their own target while the caregiver interacts with an individual animal in the group, thus eliminating the need for physical separation. Third, the target can facilitate control of fine movement by teaching the animal to touch the target with foot, arm, chest, back, or ear.

Shaping or successive approximation.   *Shaping* is the process by which behaviors are taught. Shaping consists of dividing a behavior into small increments or steps and then teaching one step at a time until the desired behavior is achieved. The key to successful shaping is the ability to identify steps that are appropriate to the behavior being trained and the animal learning it. Too large steps can create confusion and frustration in the animal. Too small steps can lead to loss of motiva-tion and boredom. The following is an example of one potential shaping plan to train the primate to present a leg for venipuncture.

1. Use a target to encourage the animal to move to the front of the cage.
2. Reinforce for staying at the target for increasing periods of time.

3. Secure the target at a height that encourages the animal to sit and reinforce when this occurs.
4. Use a second target to focus attention on desired leg; reinforce any movement of the leg towards the target.
5. Open the port in the cage and target the leg out through the opening until the leg is fully extended.
6. Reinforce for keeping the leg in that position for increasing periods of time.

Desensitization.   *Desensitization* is a highly effective training tool that can help laboratory primates tolerate and eventually accept a wide array of frightening or uncomfortable stimuli. By pairing positive rewards with any action, object, or event that causes fear, that fearful entity slowly becomes less negative, less frightening, and less stressful. Animals can be desensitized to husbandry, veterinary, and research procedures, new enclosures, the squeeze cage, unfamiliar people, negatively perceived people such as the veterinarian, novel objects, strange noises, and any other potentially aversive stimuli. Effective desensitization requires pairing many positive rewards directly with the uncomfortable or aversive experience or with a similar experience. That requires precise reinforcement so that the conditioned reinforcer (bridge) occurs at the exact moment the animal experiences the stimulus. When desensitization is done well, animals are likely to cooperate voluntarily with behaviors with little or no sign of recognizable stress or fear.

Desensitization is a very powerful, versatile, and valuable technique that should be used whenever the animal shows signs of fear or discomfort in relation to any event. In the previous shaping plan example, desensitization would train the primate to accept the actual needle piercing the skin. The following series of steps illustrate the desensitization process.

1. Touch the leg at blood collection site with a finger or blunt object; bridge when the object touches the skin and then reinforce; repeat until the animal shows no fear or discomfort; repeat desensitization process with following objects: capped syringe, a needle with the tip cut off so it is blunted, syringe with the real needle.
2. Extend the length of time the object touches the skin.
3. Desensitize the primate to the touch and smell of alcohol swab.
4. Desensitize the animal to the presence of a second person, then to the presence of the veterinarian or technician.

Cooperative feeding.   It is most desirable to house naturally social animals, like primates, in pairs or groups (de Waal, 1987). However, because of the constraints captivity imposes on animals and their ability to avoid or escape negative behavior, social housing must be carefully implemented and monitored, or it can become a stressful and even dangerous experience for subordinate animals (Coe,

1991; Crockett, 1998). Using a training technique we call *cooperative feeding,* it is possible to enhance introductions, mitigate dominance-related problems, increase affiliative behaviors, and reduce aggression in socially housed animals (Laule & Desmond, 1991). Operationally, this entails reinforcing two events within the group simultaneously: Dominant animals are reinforced for allowing subdominant animals to receive food or attention, whereas the subdominant animals are reinforced for being "brave" enough to accept food or attention in the presence of these more aggressive animals.

It is important to note that dominance is not eliminated; in fact, it is acknowledged. Aggression is a normal component of social behavior; therefore, the goal is to reduce aggression to an appropriate and acceptable level. Cooperative feeding can help ensure that all individuals—not just the stronger or more dominant ones—enjoy a quality of life. Studies have shown significant reduction of excessive aggression (Bloomsmith et al., 1994) and an increase in affiliative behaviors as a result of the training (Cox, 1987; Desmond et al., 1987; Schapiro et al., 2001; Schapiro et al., 2003/this issue).

AN ANIMAL MANAGEMENT INVENTORY

We suggest that the first step in moving toward a more positive reinforcement-based management system is to take an inventory of current practices. Identify the daily and as-needed interactions that occur between an animal and staff members. The activities may include (a) visually inspecting the animal; (b) cleaning and feeding; (c) human/animal interacting for enrichment; (d) providing food or object enrichment; (e) moving animals from one location to another; (f) introducing or separating animals; and (g) performing veterinary procedures or research protocols.

The next step is to identify the management practice (positive or negative reinforcement) used in each interaction. Are the animals provided a clear cue or signal and then given the opportunity to cooperate in the procedure in exchange for something they like (a treat, attention, verbal praise)? Are the animals "made" to cooperate through the threat of something negative (a net, squirt of water, use of a squeeze mechanism, human intimidation, or physical restraint)?

Such an inventory can yield surprises. It also is a reminder that training—whether we recognize it or not—is occurring all the time, and so is learning. Unless we are aware of what we are reinforcing, and what we are not, a lot of unwanted learning can result. The approach used to collect monthly urine samples from cycling female chimpanzees (*Pan troglodytes*) at one facility involved moving the female out of her homecage and into a clean transport cage. A caregiver would then give her juice from a squirt bottle and wait until she urinated. The longer the chimp did not urinate, the more juice she got. She was being unintentionally reinforced and, thus, "trained" to wait as long as possible before urinating.

An inventory of this kind also can reveal behaviors or negative coping strategies that are likely to be related, in some degree, to the handling practices employed. Reliance on negative reinforcement techniques can lead to avoidance, aggression, fear, self-aggression, and stereotypic behavior on the part of the animal. Given the benefits that PRT offers the animals, the staff, and the institution, it is desirable to identify specific interactions that currently are being managed through negative reinforcement and to evolve those slowly into a PRT-based approach.

EVOLVING INTO A PRT SYSTEM

Primates in the laboratory environment have unique care and management requirements, and there often are significant limitations placed on the staff to meet those needs. Usually, caregiver staff is responsible for large numbers of animals and a population that may change frequently. Often, staff is given only short periods to prepare animals for research procedures. Housing conditions vary from small caging that severely restricts the animal's range of physical movement to big corrals with large numbers of animals that are difficult to access on an individual basis. Research protocols often dictate or restrict an animal's amount and type of food, type of physical activity, ability to live in social housing, and acceptable enrichment options.

These conditions of life in the laboratory make a formal PRT program difficult to implement. However, it is feasible to integrate PRT into existing management procedures to improve the care and welfare of resident primates. To develop such a system, the following actions are recommended:

1. Provide some basic training in PRT techniques to all animal care staff. By developing staff who are familiar with these techniques and have some degree of competence in using them, the quality of care of laboratory animals can be greatly improved.

2. Incorporate PRT into interactions with animals for daily management and to gain cooperation for veterinary and research procedures. Give animals the opportunity and motivation to cooperate voluntarily in these procedures. Caregivers should provide clear cues for desired responses, and reinforce those responses when they occur.

3. Exercise patience. To increase success, give animals a reasonable opportunity to cooperate in the desired behavior.

4. Plan ahead and actively prepare animals for veterinary procedures, research protocols, or any foreseen changes in the routine such as altering social groups or environmental factors.

CONCLUSIONS

The use of PRT as an animal care and management tool offers many benefits to biomedical facilities and to their animals, staff, and researchers. It allows managers to address proactively a wide range of situations that have significant implications for animal care and welfare. Primary among these is the ability to gain the voluntary cooperation of animals in husbandry, veterinary, and research procedures. Desensitization can significantly reduce the fear and stress associated with these procedures. Training can be applied in a wide array of situations. When appropriately and skillfully applied, PRT represents a viable option to the traditional approach to the management of animals in the laboratory. Making the shift to a more positive reinforcement-based system significantly enhances the welfare of the animals.

REFERENCES

Animal Welfare Act. 52 Fed. Reg. (61). 10292–10322 (1987).

Bayne, K., Dexter, S., & Strange, D. (1993). The effects of food provisioning and human interaction on the behavioral well-being of rhesus monkeys (*Macaca mulatta*). *Contemporary Topics (AALAS), 32,* 6–9.

Bloomsmith, M. (1992). Chimpanzee training and behavioral research: A symbiotic relationship. In *Proceedings of the American Association of Zoological Parks and Aquariums Annual Conference* (pp. 403–410). Toronto, Ontario, Canada: American Association of Zoological Parks and Aquariums.

Bloomsmith, M., Lambeth, S., Stone, A., & Laule, G. (1997). Comparing two types of human interaction as enrichment for chimpanzees. *American Journal of Primatology, 42,* 96.

Bloomsmith, M. A., Laule, G. E., Alford, P. L., & Thurston, R. H. (1994). Using training to moderate chimpanzee aggression during feeding. *Zoo Biology, 13,* 557–566.

Coe, C. (1991). Is social housing of primates always the optimal choice? In M. Novak & A. Petto (Eds.), *Through the looking glass* (pp. 78–92). Washington, DC: American Psychological Association.

Cox, C. (1987). Increase in the frequency of social interactions and the likelihood of reproduction among drills. In *Proceedings of the American Association of Zoological Parks and Aquariums Western Regional Conference* (pp. 321–328). Fresno, CA: American Association of Zoological Parks and Aquariums.

Crockett, C. (1998). Psychological well-being of captive non-human primates: Lessons from the laboratory studies. In D. Shepherdson, J. Mellen, & M. Hutchins (Eds.), *Second nature: Environmental enrichment for captive animals* (pp. 129–152). Washington, DC: Smithsonian Institution Press.

de Waal, F. (1987). The social nature of primates. In M. Novak & A. Petto (Eds.), *Through the looking glass* (pp. 69–77). Washington, DC: American Psychological Association.

Desmond, T., & Laule, G. (1994). Use of positive reinforcement training in the management of species for reproduction. *Zoo Biology, 13,* 471–477.

Desmond, T., Laule, G., & McNary, J. (1987). Training for socialization and reproduction with drills. In *Proceedings of the American Association of Zoological Parks and Aquariums* (pp. 435–441). Wheeling, WV: American Association of Zoological Parks and Aquariums.

Hanson, J., Larson, M., & Snowdon, C. (1976). The effects of control over high intensity noise on plasma cortisol levels in rhesus monkeys. *Behavioural Biology, 16,* 333–340.

Kobert, M. (1997). Operant conditioning as an enrichment strategy at the San Diego Zoo. In V. J. Hare & K. E. Worley (Eds.), *Proceedings of the Third International Conference on Environmental Enrichment, Orlando, FL* (pp. 230–236). San Diego, CA: Shape of Enrichment.

Laule, G. (1993). The use of behavioural management techniques to reduce or eliminate abnormal behaviour. *Animal Welfare Information Center Newsletter, 4,* 1–11.

Laule, G., & Desmond, T. (1991). Meeting behavioral objectives while maintaining healthy social behavior and dominance—A delicate balance. In *Proceedings of the International Marine Animal Trainers Association Annual Conference* (pp. 19–25). San Francisco: International Marine Animal Trainers Association.

Laule, G., & Desmond, T. (1998). Positive reinforcement training as an enrichment strategy. In D. Shepherdson, J. Mellen, & M. Hutchins (Eds.), *Second nature: Environmental enrichment for captive animals* (pp. 302–312). Washington, DC: Smithsonian Institution Press.

Laule, G., & Whittaker, M. (2001). The use of positive reinforcement techniques with chimpanzees for enhanced care and welfare. In L. Brent (Ed.), *The care and management of captive chimpanzees* (pp. 243–266). San Antonio, TX: American Society of Primatologists.

Markowitz, H. (1982). *Behavioral enrichment in the zoo.* New York: Van Nostrand Reinhold.

McKinley, J., Buchanan-Smith, H. M., Bassett, L., & Morris K. (2003/this issue). Training common marmosets (*Callithrix jacchus*) to cooperate during routine laboratory procedures: Ease of training and time investment. *Journal of Applied Animal Welfare Science, 6,* 209–220.

Mineka, S., Gunnar, M., & Champoux, M. (1986). The effects of control in the early social and emotional development of rhesus monkeys. *Child Development, 57,* 1241–1256.

Moseley J., & Davis, J. (1989). Psychological enrichment techniques and New World monkey restraint device reduce colony management time. *Laboratory Animal Science, 39,* 31–33.

Neuringer, A. (1969). Animals respond for food in the presence of free food. *Science, 166,* 339–341.

Norton, B., Hutchins, M., Stevens, E., & Maple, T. (1995). *Ethics on the ark: Zoos, animal welfare, and wildlife conservation.* Washington, DC: Smithsonian Institution Press.

Novak, M., & Petto, A. (1991). *Through the looking glass.* Washington, DC: American Psychological Association.

Reichard, T., Shellabarger, W., & Laule, G. (1992). Training for husbandry and medical purposes. In *Proceedings of the American Association of Zoological Parks and Aquariums National Conference* (pp. 396–402). Wheeling, WV: American Association of Zoological Parks and Aquariums.

Reinhardt, V. (1992). Improved handling of experimental rhesus monkeys. In H. Davis & A. Balfour (Eds.), *The inevitable bond: Examining scientist–animal interactions* (pp. 171–177). Cambridge, England: Cambridge University Press.

Reinhardt, V. (1997). Training nonhuman primates to cooperate during handling procedures: A review. *Animal Technologist, 48,* 55–73.

Reinhardt, V., & Cowley, D. (1992). In-homecage blood collection from conscious stump tailed macaques. *Animal Welfare, 1,* 249–255.

Reinhardt, V., Cowley, D., Scheffler, J., Vertein, R., & Wegner, F. (1990). Cortisol response of female rhesus monkeys to venipuncture in homecage versus venipuncture in restraint apparatus. *Journal of Medical Primatology, 19,* 601–606.

Reinhardt, V., Liss, C., & Stevens, C. (1995). Restraint methods of laboratory non-human primates: A critical review. *Animal Welfare, 4,* 221–238.

Schapiro, S. J., Bloomsmith, M. A., & Laule, G. E. (2003/this issue). Positive reinforcement training as a technique to alter nonhuman primate behavior: Quantitative assessments of effectiveness. *Journal of Applied Animal Welfare Science, 6,* 175–187.

Schapiro, S. J., Perlman, J. E., & Boudreau, B. A. (2001). Manipulating the affiliative interactions of group-housed rhesus macaques using PRT techniques. *American Journal of Primatology, 55,* 137–149.

Segal, E. (1989). *Housing, care and psychological well-being of captive and laboratory primates.* New York: Noyes.

Shepherdson, D. J., Mellen, J. D., & Hutchins, M. E. (1998). *Second nature: Environmental enrichment for captive animals.* Washington, DC: Smithsonian Institutional Press.

Stone, A., Laule, G., Bloomsmith, M., & Alford, P. (1995). Positive reinforcement training to facilitate the medical management of captive chimpanzees. *Paper presented at the 33rd annual meeting, Texas branch of the American Association for Laboratory Animal Science*, San Antonio.

Turkkan, J., Ator, N., Brady, J., & Craven, K. (1989). Beyond chronic catheterization in laboratory primates. In E. Segal (Ed.), *Housing, care and psychological well-being of captive and laboratory primates* (pp. 305–322). New York: Noyes.

JOURNAL OF APPLIED ANIMAL WELFARE SCIENCE, 6(3), 175–187
Copyright © 2003, Lawrence Erlbaum Associates, Inc.

Positive Reinforcement Training As a Technique to Alter Nonhuman Primate Behavior: Quantitative Assessments of Effectiveness

Steven J. Schapiro

Department of Veterinary Sciences
The University of Texas M. D. Anderson Cancer Center

Mollie A. Bloomsmith

TECHLab
Zoo Atlanta, and
Yerkes National Primate Research Center
Atlanta, Georgia

Gail E. Laule

Active Environments
Lompoc, California

Many suggest that operant conditioning techniques can be applied successfully to improve the behavioral management of nonhuman primates in research settings. However, relatively little empirical data exist to support this claim. This article is a review of several studies that discussed applied positive reinforcement training techniques (PRT) on breeding/research colonies of rhesus macaques (*Macaca mulatta*) and chimpanzees (*Pan troglodytes*) at The University of Texas M. D. Anderson Cancer Center and measured their effectiveness. Empirical analyses quantified the amount of time required to train rhesus monkeys to come up, station, target, and stay. Additionally, a study found that time spent affiliating by female rhesus was changed as a function of training low affiliators to affiliate more and high affiliators to affiliate less.

Requests for reprints should be sent to Steven J. Schapiro, Department of Veterinary Sciences, The University of Texas M. D. Anderson Cancer Center, 650 Cool Water Drive, Bastrop, TX 78602. E-mail: sschapir@mdanderson.org

Another study successfully trained chimpanzees to feed without fighting and to come inside on command. PRT is an important behavioral management tool that can improve the care and welfare of primates in captivity. Published empirical findings are essential for managers to assess objectively the utility of positive reinforcement training techniques in enhancing captive management and research procedures.

This article is intended as a review of several studies (Bloomsmith, Laule, Alford, & Thurston, 1994; Bloomsmith, Stone, & Laule, 1998; Schapiro, Perlman, & Boudreau, 2001) we have conducted examining the effects of positive reinforcement training (PRT) techniques on the behavioral management of large colonies of rhesus monkeys (*Macaca mulatta*) and chimpanzees (*Pan troglodytes*) in captivity. Although many primatologists and animal trainers claim that PRT techniques can be employed effectively to facilitate the behavioral management of nonhuman primates in captivity (Desmond & Laule, 1994; Laule & Desmond, 1995; Laule & Whittaker, 2001; Reinhardt, Liss, & Stevens, 1995; Whittaker, Laule, Perlman, Schapiro, & Keeling, 2001), relatively few quantitative reports are available in the literature. Indeed, one of the aims of this special issue of the *Journal of Applied Animal Welfare Science (JAAWS)* is to rectify this situation.

The primary goal of this article is to provide empirical data assessing the "effectiveness" and "value" of PRT techniques. Some of the most frequently asked questions concerning PRT include, "How long does it take to train behavior X?" and "What effects does training have on the behavior of the primates?" Therefore, for the purposes of this article, *effectiveness* will include measures of the time required to train desired behaviors and/or measures of the behavioral effects of training procedures.

PRT techniques are one type of behavioral management procedure that can be applied successfully and beneficially to many aspects of both the management of primates in captivity and their use in research (Bloomsmith et al., 1994; Desmond & Laule, 1994; Laule & Desmond, 1995; Laule, Thurston, Alford, & Bloomsmith, 1996; Laule & Whittaker, 2001; Reinhardt et al., 1995; Schapiro et al., 2001; Vertein & Reinhardt, 1989; Whittaker et al., 2001). PRT techniques are simply standard operant conditioning techniques in which animals, presented with a stimulus, perform a target behavior and subsequently receive a desired reward. These techniques allow the animals to cooperate voluntarily with husbandry and/or research procedures. See Laule and Whittaker (2001) and some of the contributions in this special edition for additional recent discussions of the methods of PRT.

Training primates in captive (including laboratory) settings to perform target behaviors that facilitate husbandry, veterinary procedures, and/or research protocols is possible and desirable (Laule & Desmond, 1995; Laule et al., 1996; Laule & Whittaker, 2001; Reinhardt, 1997; Reinhardt et al., 1995; Schapiro et al., 2001). The interaction of many factors, including facility design; housing conditions; research protocols; and animal characteristics (species, age, sex, rearing history) will help determine the specific target behaviors of the PRT program (Laule & Whittaker, 2001). There are relatively few captive situations in which PRT would be of no value to the primates or to those managing them.

This article reviews three previously published projects and one unpublished project. For the three previously published projects, the article presents only the basic elements of the procedures and results of the studies, referring the reader to the original reports (Bloomsmith et al., 1994; Bloomsmith et al., 1998; Schapiro et al., 2001) for additional details. For the unpublished study, the article presents more of the essential details of the procedures and results. All four studies demonstrate the potential contributions of PRT techniques to effective behavioral management and research programs.

METHODS AND RESULTS

Study 1: Training Rhesus Monkeys to Stay; Time Investment

Methods.   The first study presented is unpublished and was designed to address issues related to quantifying the investment of personnel time required to train rhesus monkeys living in small groups (one male and five to seven females) to perform certain target/control behaviors. The target activities discussed are basic; yet, they provide a foundation of trained behaviors that facilitate the training of other, more complex and valuable behaviors.

Thirty adult rhesus monkeys of both sexes (3 males, 27 females) were trained while living in 5 unimale-multifemale groups in kennel-type runs (2.4 × 3.0 × 2.7 m); two of the males purposely were not trained; Schapiro et al. (1997) provide additional details concerning housing. Subjects were part of the specific pathogen-free (SPF) breeding colony at The University of Texas M. D. Anderson Cancer Center's Department of Veterinary Sciences and had participated in a number of other behavioral and/or immunological investigations (Buchl, Keeling, & Voss, 1997; Schapiro, 2002; Schapiro et al., 1994). Monkeys were clicker trained (Laule, Bloomsmith, & Schapiro, 2003/this issue) and then trained to perform four progressively more difficult behaviors (up, station, target, stay) using PRT techniques. Other articles in this issue provide additional details on conditioned reinforcers. Most training sessions were 15 min in duration, and groups participated in approximately 3 training sessions per week, each group being trained by a single trainer. No individuals were separated from their groups during training; therefore, training was conducted within the constraints imposed by the social hierarchy of rhesus groups. Typically, this meant that dominant individuals were reinforced not only for performing their target behaviors but also for allowing subordinate animals to receive their reinforcers. This issue will be addressed in more detail in the section devoted to cooperative feeding (Bloomsmith et al., 1994; Desmond, Laule, & McNary, 1987) presented below. A subject was considered reliably trained for one of the target behaviors when that monkey performed the behavior in three consecutive training sessions. Although the data are presented as the mean training time required per monkey to achieve reliable performance, it should be pointed out that this refers to the amount of time that the monkey's group was trained, not the amount of time that each monkey was trained.

The first trained behavior, "up," simply involved the monkeys' coming up to the front of the cage on command. Whereas monkeys would perform many of the target behaviors at times, one of the key issues in PRT is to put desired behaviors under some degree of stimulus control. This means that the animals reliably perform the behavior when requested to do so.

The second trained behavior, "station," required each monkey to approach an individual station (a uniquely shaped and positioned PVC target mounted on the cage front) on command. "Target" was the third behavior in the sequence, requiring the monkeys to touch their individual targets with a hand (again, on command). Finally, monkeys were trained to "stay," holding their target and/or not moving from their stations until verbally released by the trainer.

Results.   Twenty-seven of the 30 monkeys were reliably trained (performed the behavior during 3 consecutive training sessions) to come up to the front of the cage on command after their group had received a mean of 2.5 hr of training. The fastest monkey took only 25 min to meet the criterion for this task, whereas the slowest took over 16 hr (see Table 1). Twenty-two of the monkeys took less than 2 hr to learn the behavior, whereas 3 animals never met criterion.

Monkeys were trained to station in a mean of just under 3 hr of total training time (see Table 1). This included the 2.5 hr (on average) spent learning the up command. The fastest monkey was stationing in just under 1 hr and 20 monkeys reliably stationed after less than 2 hr of training time. Only one of the 27 monkeys who were successfully trained to come up, could not be trained to station.

Twenty-four of the 26 monkeys who were successfully trained to station also were reliably trained to touch their targets on command. A mean of slightly more than 5 hr of total training time was required to meet criterion for this behavior (see Table 1). The fastest monkey required only 55 min to achieve reliability, and 14 monkeys were trained to criterion in less than 3.5 hr. Therefore, once monkeys had been trained to come up and to station, it took a mean of only an additional 2 hr to train them to target.

The next behavior in the progression, stay, presented an interesting challenge. Fourteen of the 24 targeting animals required absolutely no training to stay. Once at their targets, these typically lower ranking animals simply stayed. The other 10

TABLE 1
The Number of Hours Required to Train Rhesus Monkeys to Reliably Perform the Target
Behaviors on Command

Target Behavior	Up	Station	Target	Stay
Number of hours of training required to meet criterion				
0 to 1	5	5	1	0
1 to 2	17	15	6	2
2 to 3	1	1	4	5
3 to 4	1	1	3	0
4 to 5	0	0	4	5
5 to 10	1	2	2	5
10+	2	2	4	7
M[a]	2.5	3.0	5.0	9.5[b]
Mode[a]	1.1	1.1	2.0	2[b]
Mdn[a]	1.2	2.0	3.2	6.8[b]
Subjects successfully trained	27/30	26/27	24/26	24/24

Note.   Entries in the table indicate the number of subjects successfully trained during the time period.
[a]Given in hours. [b]14 subjects required no additional training to stay. Mean, mode, and median values refer only to those 10 subjects who required training to stay.

animals however, required considerable training (at least 4.5 additional hours, see Table 1) to achieve reliability for stay. These were the animals, typically higher ranking individuals, who would attempt to leave their targets and steal the reinforcers intended for other animals. Although stay is relatively difficult to train, it is an extremely valuable behavior for both management and research purposes, significantly increasing access to all animals in the group.

Study 2: Training Rhesus Monkeys; Affiliative Interactions

Methods.   This study has been previously published (Schapiro et al., 2001) and was designed to use PRT techniques to manipulate prospectively the amount of time that adult female rhesus monkeys engaged in affiliative interactions. As increased levels of affiliative interactions have been correlated with enhanced immune responses (Capitanio, Mendoza, Lerche, & Mason, 1998; Kaplan et al., 1991), we felt this was an interesting relationship to explore. In brief, 28 group-housed subjects in the rhesus SPF breeding colony were identified as either high affiliators or low affiliators, based on a median split of the time they spent engaged in affiliative activities (social play, social grooming) during a baseline observation period (250 hr of focal animal data). Half of the 14 low affiliators were trained to affiliate, and half of the high affiliators then were trained not to affiliate (as a positive control condition), using PRT techniques. The rest of the animals, not trained, served as control subjects.

High affiliators were trained not to affiliate by training the monkeys to target and stay (as in Study 1) at targets that were gradually moved from within a social distance (< 8 cm) of another monkey to outside of a social distance (> 8 cm) of all other monkeys. Low affiliators, on the other hand, were trained to affiliate by training them to target and stay at targets that gradually were moved from outside a social distance of all other monkeys to within a social distance of a single partner monkey. Low affiliators then were trained, through the shaping of successive approximations, to place their hands on the back of the partner and simulate grooming-like hand movements. Schapiro et al. (2001) provide additional details on the training procedures and experimental design of this study. After the baseline period, subjects were observed both during (trained subjects only) and outside of training sessions (an additional 340 hr of focal animal data).

Results.   PRT aimed at altering the affiliative interactions of socially housed, adult female rhesus macaques altered the affiliative behavior patterns of both high affiliators and low affiliators (see Table 2). In general, high affiliators were successfully trained not to affiliate, spending significantly less time affiliating during the training phase (a) than they did during the baseline phase, $t(5) = 5.5, p < .01$, and (b) than did untrained high affiliators during the training phase of the study, $F(1, 10) = 9.3, p < .05$. These data suggest that high affiliators were responding to the reinforcement contingencies of the training process yet were not altering their overall behavioral repertoire. Low affiliators were successfully trained to affiliate more (12.5% of observation time) during observations outside of training sessions, $t(6) = -2.14, p < .08$, than during the baseline phase (6.7%). This suggested that, unlike trained high affiliators, the overall behavioral repertoires of these subjects were altered as a function of PRT (the difference approached significance). For additional details concerning the results of this study, see Schapiro et al. (2001).

TABLE 2
Mean Percentage of Observation Time Spent Affiliating With Adult Rhesus Monkeys Across Study Phases (Baseline Versus Training), Experimental Conditions (Trained Versus Untrained), and Observation Times (During Training Versus Outside of Training)

		Training Phase	
Subgroup	Baseline Phase	During Training	Outside Training
Trained high affiliators	17.9	2.9	14.3
Untrained high affiliators	15.1	—	13.7
Trained low affiliators	6.7	4.5	12.5
Untrained low affiliators	8.2	—	11.2

Note.   Complete data set can be found in Schapiro, Perlman, and Boudreau (2001).

Study 3: Training to Moderate Chimpanzee
Feeding-Related Aggression

Methods.   This study has been previously published (Bloomsmith et al., 1994) and was designed to measure the effect of a cooperative feeding paradigm (Desmond et al., 1987) on the amount of aggression during feeding in a relatively large group of chimpanzees. Our chimpanzee research colony contains approximately 160 animals housed in a variety of social settings including pairs, trios, small groups (4 to 6 animals), and large groups (7 to 16 animals). Facilities with both indoor and outdoor components house all animals. Most pairs and trios live in run-type enclosures, most small groups in Primadomes, and most large groups in corrals (Riddle, Keeling, Alford, & Beck, 1982).

In some groups of chimpanzees, certain dominant animals routinely chase more subordinate animals and steal their portion of food. This creates many problems; including dominant animals who may become overweight and subordinate animals who may not receive proper nutrition. The group we studied had such a dominant animal. Although it is difficult to use PRT techniques to train a chimpanzee not to do an undesirable behavior, it is considerably easier to train that animal to perform a behavior that is incompatible with the undesirable behavior (Laule & Whittaker, 2001). The process of training for cooperative feeding involves exactly this procedure. To train dominant animals not to chase and steal subordinates' food, the dominants are reinforced for sitting in one spot, a behavior incompatible with chasing and stealing. In essence, as alluded to briefly in Study 1, dominant animals are reinforced for allowing subordinate animals to receive their food ration.

Considerable details on cooperative feeding are available in Bloomsmith et al. (1994); in general, however, dominant animals initially are given the verbal stimulus, "sit," and are reinforced for doing so. As training progresses, these same animals are asked to sit while the other animals in the group are fed their rations and are reinforced for doing so. Eventually, the animals who remain sitting while allowing the other animals in the group to receive their food receive a high value reinforcer (an apple) in addition to their regular food items. The data included in the older report (Bloomsmith et al., 1994) included eight subjects. Currently, all 90 subjects living in our corrals generally feed without fighting, although not all groups required PRT to accomplish this.

Results.   Training a group of chimpanzees using the cooperative feeding procedure resulted in significant changes in feeding-related agonistic behavior before and after training, $F(1,6) = 15.5$, $p < .05$. Aggressive, display, submissive, and reconciliatory behaviors all showed similar patterns of decline. These findings applied to incidents involving the target male as well as to the group as a whole (see Table 3). Levels of the behaviors included in Table 3 at times other than meal periods did not change as a function of training. These results indicate that the training

TABLE 3
Means and Standard Error Rates (Per Hour) of Agonistic Behaviors Among Chimpanzees
During the Four Study Conditions

| | Pretraining | | | | Posttraining | | | |
| | No Meal | | Meal | | No Meal | | Meal | |
Study Condition	M	SE	M	SE	M	SE	M	SE
Behavior								
Display								
Group[a]	0.9	1.5	6.6	5.1	2.4	2.2	1.4	1.4
Male	0.5		4.4		1.3		0.6	
Aggressive								
Group	0.6	1.1	7.7	5.7	0.9	0.9	1.7	1.7
Male	0.4		2.7		0.2		0.7	
Submissive								
Group	3.7	5.7	22.3	15.4	5.4	4.5	0.4	0.5
Male	0.1		0.0		0.0		0.0	
Reconciliation								
Group	1.0	1.2	2.7	3.0	0.4	0.5	0.3	0.5
Male	0.1		0.4		0.0		0.0	

Note.   Complete data set can be found in Bloomsmith, Laule, Alford, and Thurston (1994).
[a]Group scores are for all eight group members combined, including the target male.

process decreased agonism to levels equivalent to nonfeeding times of the day, thereby eliminating the additional aggression that had been evident when meals were fed. For more details concerning the results of this study, see Bloomsmith et al. (1994).

Study 4: Training for Chimpanzee Voluntary Movement

Methods.   This study has been previously published (Bloomsmith et al., 1998) and was designed to measure the effort required to train chimpanzees to reliably come into the indoor portion of their corral enclosure when asked to do so. A critical component of any behavioral management program is to be able to move animals from one section of their enclosure to another section on command (typically referred to as "shifting" or "gating"). This is accomplished best using standard operant conditioning procedures whereby the animals are asked to come inside and are reinforced with juice, fruit, and/or other treats when they come inside and the door is closed behind them (a training attempt). If 100% of the animals in the group complied, then the training attempt was equivalent to a training session. If less than 100% of the animals in the group complied during a training attempt, an additional attempt was made.

In this case, the training session was comprised of multiple-training attempts. Sixty-six chimpanzees were observed for this four-phase study, and we measured the percentage compliance of the subjects with the command, inside, during each phase. During the baseline phase, subjects received no reinforcement for coming inside when called by the trainer. During the initial training phase, subjects received positive reinforcement from the trainer for coming inside when called by the trainer. The initial training phase continued until 90% compliance was reached, at which point the maintenance phase of the study began. The maintenance phase also employed the trainers providing the stimulus and the reinforcement and continued until the transfer phase began. During the transfer phase, a member of the caregiving staff, rather than the trainer, called the animals in, reinforced them, and worked the doors. For additional details concerning the precise methodology of this study, see Bloomsmith et al. (1998).

Results.   Means of 16.1 training sessions and 22 training attempts were required to reach the 90% criterion for successful training of the inside behavior (see Table 4). On average, a training attempt lasted less than 5 min; therefore, less than 110 min were typically required to train a group to criterion. There was considerable variability in the number of sessions required to reach reliability ($SE = 17.8$; range = 4 to 93). Females ($M = 11.6$) required significantly fewer, $F(1, 64) = 6.0, p < .02$, training sessions than did males ($M = 25$). Compliance differed significantly across phases of the study, and adult males were the poorest performers across all phases. There were no age effects or age by sex interactions. Compliance (89.8%) during the first 55 attempts at the beginning of the transfer phase was significantly lower, $F(1, 64) = 9.1, p < .004$, than compliance (94.2%) during the 20 final attempts of the maintenance phase. Although this difference is statistically significant, the compliance rate early in the transfer phase still is well above the baseline

TABLE 4
Percentage Compliance Scores for Chimpanzees Across Study Phases

Study Phase	Baseline[a]	Initial Training[a]	Maintenance Training[b]	Transfer of Training[b]
Subjects				
Adult females	77.9	88.7	95.8	94.2
Adult males	41.6	70.0	84.7	76.2
Immature females	65.4	81.9	87.7	87.2
Immature males	66.1	78.9	93.1	84.2
M all subjects	66.1	82.1	91.7	87.9
Total number of attempts				
for individuals	942	1,451	2,181	8,128

Note.   Complete data set can be found in Bloomsmith, Stone, and Laule (1998).
[a]$n = 66$. [b]$n = 58$.

compliance level (see Table 4). For additional details concerning the results of this study, see Bloomsmith et al. (1998).

DISCUSSION

The primary goal of this brief review was to provide the reader with examples of studies of PRT that empirically measured the effectiveness of these techniques. For the purposes of this article, two specific measures of effectiveness were emphasized: (a) the amount of time required to train particular behaviors, and (b) the behavioral changes resulting from training. These specific measures of effectiveness should provide managers of primates in captivity with the information needed to assess the value of implementing positive reinforcement training techniques in their management and research programs.

The data included from the four studies discussed above emphasize the potential value of PRT to the captive management, well-being, and research utilization of nonhuman primates (Laule & Whittaker, 2001; Whittaker et al., 2001) and provide some of the empirical data necessary to evaluate the effectiveness of such procedures. The combined data from these four studies clearly indicate that PRT techniques can be used effectively to achieve both management and research goals. Although some behaviors are more difficult to train than others, it is clear that both desirable and undesirable behaviors can be manipulated using these techniques. Even affiliative and agonistic interaction patterns can be influenced, demonstrating the power of PRT techniques to alter even some of the most critical species-typical activities in the primates' behavioral repertoire. Although cooperative feeding is not a requirement for housing chimpanzees in large social groups, PRT aimed at minimizing aggression at meal times can only benefit the animals and those who manage them.

Two aspects of the present findings deserve special attention in this article. The first is the concept of training an incompatible behavior as a mechanism for facilitating the elimination of undesirable behaviors from primates' activity patterns. Although we addressed this primarily in the context of cooperative feeding (Bloomsmith et al., 1994; Desmond et al., 1987), there are many other circumstances in which the preferential reinforcement of desirable behaviors that cannot be performed at the same time as undesirable behaviors can be used to eliminate those undesirable behaviors from the animals' behavioral repertoire. One way to minimize primates' grabbing their caregivers (and thereby minimize risks to human safety) is to reinforce the animals for stationing and targeting with their hands on their perches inside their cages. Of course, this approach will not work for every animal or every undesirable behavior.

The second point worthy of emphasis from the cumulative findings of this article relates to the challenges inherent in attempting to train intelligent, socially oriented animals, like primates, without separating them from their social groups. Separating animals from their groups can be a time consuming process; more important, it can be stressful for both those removed and those remaining behind. Therefore, we prefer to work with intact social groups, even when the objective is to gain access to, and train, a single animal for a particular behavior (such as urine collection).

When working with groups of animals and the associated complex social dynamics, it often is easier to train certain group members than others. In some situations, "highly trainable" subsets of animals can be identified (e.g., female chimpanzees to come inside; lower ranking rhesus monkeys to stay as described previously), but this is not always the case. For commands such as station and inside, management goals have not been completely achieved unless all animals station or come inside. In other words, the amount of training time required per group may not be distributed evenly within the group; some animals may require only one or two sessions, whereas others may require many, many sessions or may never perform the behavior.

These animals may have learned the behavior but may be unwilling to perform it within the social context of the group. Similarly, the behavioral effects of training may not be equivalent across subjects. Some animals may benefit from increased proximity to group mates or from increased access to desirable food items, whereas others may find such new circumstances additionally stressful. For these, and other related reasons, often it is difficult to provide straightforward answers to the following questions: (a) How long does it take to train behavior X? and (b) What are the effects of training behavior X?

Well-designed studies should be published and should involve (a) appropriate experimental techniques, (b) sufficient numbers of subjects, and (c) suitable quantities of data to permit generalization across different species and settings. Although people always want to know how long it takes to train particular behaviors, and this article provides some empirical data to address this question, the answer rarely is as simple as it seems and typically requires considerable detail and explanation.

ACKNOWLEDGMENTS

Financial support for parts of the projects came from NIH/NCRR Grants U42–RR05080 and U42–RR03589 to M. E. Keeling, R01–RR05092 and R01–RR03578 to M. A. Bloomsmith, and from the Biomedical Resources Foundation to S. J. Schapiro. Expert observational, training, and technical support for this work was provided by Jaine Perlman, Susan Lambeth, Debra Machamer, Adam Stone, Bob Thurston, Steve Ross, and Brock Boudreau. The positive reinforcement training program was devised in collaboration with M. E. Keeling. Thanks to the University of Texas M. D. Anderson Cancer Center primate and chimpanzee sections' veterinary and caregiving staffs for maintaining the animals in exceptional condition. Animals were maintained in facilities approved by the Association for Assessment and Accreditation for Laboratory Animal Care International and in accordance with current United States Department of Agriculture, Department of Health and Human Services, and National Institutes of Health regulations and standards. All experimental protocols were approved by the Institutional Animal Care and Use Committee of The University of Texas M. D. Anderson Cancer Center or the Yerkes National Primate Research Center of Emory University. Thanks to H. M. Buchanan-Smith and M. J. Prescott for helpful comments on an earlier version of this manuscript.

REFERENCES

Bloomsmith, M. A., Laule, G. E., Alford, P. L., & Thurston, R. H. (1994). Using training to moderate chimpanzee aggression during feeding. *Zoo Biology, 13,* 557–566.
Bloomsmith, M. A., Stone, A. M., & Laule, G. E. (1998). Positive reinforcement training to enhance the voluntary movement of group-housed chimpanzees. *Zoo Biology, 17,* 333–341.
Buchl, S. J., Keeling, M. E., & Voss, W. R. (1997). Establishing specific pathogen-free (SPF) nonhuman primate colonies. *ILAR Journal, 38*(1), 22–27.
Capitanio, J. P., Mendoza, S. P., Lerche, N. W., & Mason, W. A. (1998). Social stress results in altered glucocorticoid regulation and shorter survival in simian acquired immune deficiency syndrome. *Proceedings of the National Academy of Sciences, USA, 95,* 4714–4719.
Desmond, T., & Laule, G. (1994). Use of positive reinforcement training in the management of species for reproduction. *Zoo Biology, 13,* 471–477.
Desmond, T., Laule, G., & McNary, J. (1987). Training for socialization and reproduction with drills. In *Proceedings of the American Association of Zoological Parks and Aquariums* (pp. 435–441). Wheeling, WV: American Association of Zoological Parks and Aquariums.
Kaplan, J. R., Heise, E. R., Manuck, S. B., Shively, C. A., Cohen, S., Rabin, B. S., et al. (1991). The relationship of agonistic and affiliative behavior patterns to cellular immune function among cynomolgus monkeys (*Macaca fascicularis*) living in unstable social groups. *American Journal of Primatology, 25,* 157–173.
Laule, G. E., Bloomsmith, M. A., & Schapiro, S. J. (2003/this issue). The use of positive reinforcement training techniques to enhance the care, management, and welfare of laboratory primates. *Journal of Applied Animal Welfare Science, 6,* 163–173.
Laule, G., & Desmond, T. (1995). Use of positive reinforcement techniques to enhance animal care, research, and well-being. In K. A. L. Bayne & M. D. Kreger (Eds.), *Wildlife mammals as research models: In the laboratory and field* (pp. 53–59). Bethesda, MD: Scientists Center for Animal Welfare.
Laule, G. E., Thurston, R. H., Alford, P. L., & Bloomsmith, M. A. (1996). Training to reliably obtain blood and urine samples from a young, diabetic chimpanzee (*Pan troglodytes*). *Zoo Biology, 15,* 587–591.
Laule, G., & Whittaker, M. (2001). The use of positive reinforcement techniques with chimpanzees for enhanced care and welfare. In L. Brent (Ed.), *The care and management of captive chimpanzees* (pp. 243–266). San Antonio, TX: American Society of Primatologists.
Reinhardt, V. (1997). Training nonhuman primates to cooperate during blood collection: A review. *Laboratory Primate Newsletter, 36,* 1–4.

Reinhardt, V., Liss, C., & Stevens, C. (1995). Restraint methods of laboratory non-human primates: A critical review. *Animal Welfare, 4,* 221–238.

Riddle, K. E., Keeling, M. E., Alford, P. L., & Beck, T. F. (1982). Chimpanzee holding, rehabilitation and breeding: facilities design and colony management. *Laboratory Animal Science, 32,* 525–533.

Schapiro, S. J. (2002). Effects of social manipulations and environmental enrichment on behavior and cell-mediated immune responses in rhesus macaques. *Pharmacology, Biochemistry and Behavior, 73,* 271–278.

Schapiro, S. J., Bloomsmith, M. A., Suarez, S. A., & Porter, L. M. (1997). A comparison of the effects of simple versus complex environmental enrichment on the behaviour of group-housed, subadult rhesus macaques. *Animal Welfare, 6,* 17–28.

Schapiro, S. J., Lee-Parritz, D. E., Taylor, L. L., Watson, L., Bloomsmith, M. A., & Petto, A. (1994). Behavioral management of specific pathogen-free (SPF) rhesus macaques: Group formation, reproduction, and parental competence. *Laboratory Animal Science, 44,* 229–234.

Schapiro, S. J., Perlman, J. E., & Boudreau, B. A. (2001). Manipulating the affiliative interactions of group-housed rhesus macaques using positive reinforcement training techniques. *American Journal of Primatology, 55,* 137–149.

Vertein, R., & Reinhardt, V. (1989). Training female rhesus monkeys to cooperate during in-homecage venipuncture. *Laboratory Primate Newsletter, 28*(2), 1–3.

Whittaker, M., Laule, G., Perlman, J., Schapiro, S., & Keeling, M. (2001). A behavioral management approach to caring for Great Apes. In *Conference proceedings The apes: Challenges for the 21st century,* (pp. 131–134). Chicago: Chicago Zoological Society.

JOURNAL OF APPLIED ANIMAL WELFARE SCIENCE, 6(3), 189–197
Copyright © 2003, Lawrence Erlbaum Associates, Inc.

Working With Rather Than Against Macaques During Blood Collection

Viktor Reinhardt

Animal Welfare Institute
Washington, D.C.

Training macaques to cooperate during blood collection is a practicable and safe alternative to the traditional procedure implying forced restraint. It takes a cumulative total of about 1 hr to train an adult female or adult male rhesus macaque successfully to present a leg voluntarily and accept venipuncture in the homecage. Cooperative animals do not show the significant cortisol response and defensive reactions that typically occur in animals who are forcibly restrained during this common procedure.

Blood collection is probably the most common handling procedure nonhuman primates are subjected to in research institutions. Traditionally, it is accomplished by forcibly restraining the subject because it is believed that "all monkeys are dangerous" (Ackerley & Stones, 1969, p. 207), that "nonhuman primates can be very difficult and even dangerous to handle," and that "restraint is therefore necessary and desirable to protect both the investigator and the animal" (Robbins, Zwick, Leedy, & Stearns, 1986, p. 68). Indeed, a subdued monkey will try to show self-defensive aggression. Therefore, "despite rigorous observance of all precautions, bites and scratches are frequent" (Valerio et al., 1969, p. 45; Zakaria, Lerche, Chomel, & Kass, 1996).

THE VARIABLE

Because of "adverse conditioning or fear" (Robbins, Zwick, Leedy, & Stearns, 1986, p. 68) enforced restraint during blood collection is an extremely alarming situation (see Figure 1) that affects physiological equilibrium, thereby increasing

Requests for reprints should be sent to Viktor Reinhardt, 6014 Palmer Drive, Weed, CA 96094. E-mail: viktorawi@siskiyou.net

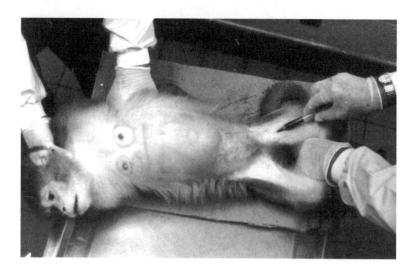

FIGURE 1   Traditional blood collection procedure.

data variability and the number of research subjects needed to achieve statistically significant results (Brockway, Hassler, & Hicks, 1993). It has been shown that compulsory restraint changes normative:

1. Cortisol secretion in rhesus (Elvidge, Challis, Robinson, Roper, & Thorburn, 1976; Fuller, Hobson, Reyes, Winter, & Faiman, 1984; Hayashi & Moberg, 1987; Line, Markowitz, Morgan, & Strong, 1991; Puri, Puri, & Anand-Kumar, 1981) and Japanese macaques (Torii, Kitagawa, Nigi, & Ohsawa, 1993) as well as in capuchin monkeys (Dettmer, Phillips, Rager, Bernstein, & Fragaszy, 1996);

2. Progesterone secretion in baboons (Albrecht, Nightingale, & Townsley, 1978; Goncharov et al., 1979);

3. Testosterone secretion in rhesus macaques (Hayashi & Moberg, 1987; Puri, Puri, & Anand-Kumar, 1981) and baboons (Goncharov et al., 1979);

4. Adrenal androgen secretion in rhesus macaques (Fuller, Hobson, Reyes, Winter, & Faiman, 1984);

5. Prolactin secretion in rhesus macaques (Quadri, Pierson, & Spies, 1978);

6. Growth hormone secretion in rhesus macaques (Mason et al., 1968);

7. Follicle stimulating hormone secretion in rhesus macaques (Todd et al., 1999);

8. Glucagon secretion in squirrel monkeys (Myers, Mendoza, & Cornelius, 1988);

9. Glucose regulation in rhesus, stump-tailed (Streett & Jonas, 1982) and Celebes macaques (Yasuda, Wolff, & Howard, 1988);

10. Serum glutamic-oxalacetic transaminase activity in rhesus macaques (Cope & Polis, 1959);

11. Aspartate aminotransferase and alanine aminotransferase activity in long-tailed macaques (Landi, Kissinger, Campbell, Kenney, & Jenkins, 1990);

12. White blood cell count in rhesus macaques (Ives & Dack, 1956; Loomis, Henrickson, & Anderson, 1980) and baboons (Goosen, Davies, Maree, & Dormehl, 1984);

13. Blood concentration in rhesus macaques (Loomis, Henrickson, & Anderson, 1980);

14. Blood pressure and heart rate in rhesus macaques (Golub & Anderson, 1986) and marmosets (Schnell & Wood, 1993);

15. Acid-base balance in squirrel monkeys (Manning, Lehner, Feldner, & Bullock, 1969) and Barbary and lion-tailed macaques (Bush, Custer, Smeller, & Bush, 1977); and

16. Respiration rate in rhesus and long-tailed macaques (Berendt & Williams, 1971).

Surprisingly, traditional blood sampling is officially "expected to produce little or no discomfort" (Scientists Center for Animal Welfare, 1987, p. 12). In line with this, many investigators tacitly ignore their subjects' stress responses during blood collection (Reinhardt & Reinhardt, 2000).

THE REFINEMENT

In an attempt to reduce the stress reaction during blood collection, six individually caged adult (8 to 12 years old) female rhesus macaques (*Macaca mulatta*) were trained to cooperate during femoral venipuncture in the homecage (see Figure 2). The subjects were used to being immobilized on a table for this procedure (see Figure 1).

The effect of the training was assessed by drawing two blood samples—the first at 13:15 ±1 min and the second at 13:30 ±1 min—from each animal during the conventional procedure involving forced restraint and, on another day, during the refined procedure involving voluntary cooperation. The animals lived in 70 cm × 75 cm × 77 cm large upper row cages. They were fed commercial dry food at 7:30 and fruit at 15:00. The macaques were subjected to no external disturbance—including personnel walking in the hallways—for 1.5 hr before the first blood drawing at 13:15. Both during the conventional and during the refined procedure, venipuncture occurred 60 to 90 sec after the caretaker had entered the animal room. The time lapse did not differ between the two conditions (conventional 76 ± 12 sec vs. refined 73 ± 14 sec; $t = 0.399$, $df = 5$, $p > .1$).

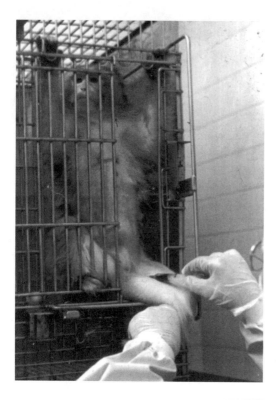

FIGURE 2   Refined blood collection procedure.

The blood samples were analyzed for serum cortisol as an indicator of stress. The first samples were used to assess basal levels; the second samples served to evaluate the magnitude of the cortisol response 15 min after venipuncture.

Mean cortisol concentrations of the first samples did not differ under both conditions, $t = 0.226$, $df = 5$, $p > .1$ (Table 1). Cortisol concentrations of the second samples, however, were significantly higher under the restraint condition than under the cooperation condition, $t = 3.910$, $df = 5$, $p < .005$ (Table 1). The magnitude of the endocrine response to venipuncture was significant (+68%), $t = 4.834$, $df = 5$, $p < .001$, when the subjects were restrained, but it was insignificant (+14%), $t = 1.135$, $df = 5$, $p > .1$, when they cooperated (see Table 1).

THE TRAINING PROTOCOL

The following protocol was used to train the subjects of this study as well as 12 adult pair-housed female, 5 adult single-housed male, 10 adult pair-housed male rhesus macaques, and 6 adult pair-housed female stump-tailed macaques (*M.*

TABLE 1
Cortisol Responses of Six Rhesus Macaques to Traditional and Refined Blood Collection

Blood Sampling Procedure	Mean Cortisol Concentrations		Difference (Significance)
	First Sample	Second Sample	
Traditional (restraint)	20.1 ± 4.5 µg/dl	33.8 ± 5.3 µg/dl	$p < .001$
Refined (cooperation)	19.6 ± 3.0 µg/dl	22.3 ± 5.0 µg/dl	$p < .1$

arctoides). The animals were used to being immobilized mechanically in their homecages during routine procedures such as ketamine injection.

Step 1

Establish an affectionate relationship with the trainee. She or he should come to the front of the cage—rather than retreat to the back—when you enter the room. The subject must trust you; only then will it be safe to proceed with the training.

Step 2

With the help of the squeeze-back, the subject is confined in the front quarter of the cage. In this position, freedom of movement is considerably restricted, but the subject has enough leeway to turn around. The animal is reassuringly talked to, gently scratched through the mesh, and offered some raisins. After a minute or two, the squeeze-back is pushed back and raisins again are offered. This exercise is repeated on different days until the animal is relaxed and accepts the food reward.

Step 3

The subject again is restricted and enticed with raisins and/or gently prodded to face the left or right side of the cage. The subject's leg is touched and groomed through the opening of the door. After a minute or two, the squeeze-back is pushed back and raisins offered. This sequence of events is repeated on different days until the animal stops retracting the leg and accepts the food reward.

Step 4

The restricted subject's leg is gently and firmly pulled through the opening of the door and held firmly for about 1 minute. The squeeze-back is pushed back and the subject rewarded with raisins. The goal of Step 4 is achieved when the animal shows no signs of resistance such a trying to retract the leg or to turn around.

Step 5

The squeeze-back is pulled only so far as to prompt the trainee to come forward. The animal is in full control of the situation and has enough room to turn around freely and avoid being touched. The trainer encouragingly asks the subject to present a leg behind or through the opening of the door. An animal who refuses to cooperate is not punished in any manner but simply does not receive a food reward. This exercise is repeated on different days until the animal actively presents a leg and shows no resistance during blood collection from the femoral vein (see Figure 2) or saphenous vein. Once this goal is achieved, the animal is praised and rewarded with raisins.

The training protocol outlined here was applied successfully not only by the author but also by two animal caretakers, Vertein (Vertein & Reinhardt, 1989) and Cowley (Reinhardt & Cowley, 1992).

THE TIME INVESTMENT

The total number of training sessions per animal ranged from 2 to 27. Individual training sessions lasted from a few seconds to 5 minutes, depending on the trainee's responsiveness. Cumulative time to reach the training goal (Step 5) ranged from 16 to 69 min with a mean of 38.5 min (see Table 2). There was a tendency, statistically insignificant, for pair-housed subjects requiring less training time than single-housed subjects; female rhesus: $t = 0.621$, $df = 16$, $p > .1$; male rhesus: $t = 0.469$, $df = 13$, $p > .1$ (Table 2). Females and males did not differ in the time needed to train them; rhesus pair-housed: $t = 0.025$, $df = 20$, $p > .1$; rhesus single-housed: $t = 0.065$, $df = 9$, $p > .1$ (see Table 2).

Although traditional blood sampling procedures usually require at least two people—one to help restrain the subject, one to puncture a vein and draw blood

TABLE 2
Time Investment to Achieve Active Cooperation of Macaques During Blood Collection in the Familiar Homecage

Subject, Housing	n	Time Investment (Minutes)
Female rhesus, single-housed	6	44.3 ± 16.6
Female rhesus, pair-housed	12	39.0 ± 18.0
Male rhesus, single-housed	5	43.6 ± 18.7[a]
Male rhesus, pair-housed	10	38.8 ± 18.6[a]
Female stump-tailed, pair-housed	6	33.5 ± 10.0[b]

[a]Data originally published in Reinhardt (1991). [b]Data originally published in Reinhardt and Cowley (1992).

(see Figure 1)—only one person is required to do this procedure with a trained subject (see Figure 2). Once trained, all animals cooperated not only with the trainer but also with the attending care personnel as well as with experienced personnel from other facilities.

CONCLUSIONS

Training macaques to cooperate voluntarily during blood collection is a practical alternative to the traditional procedure implying forced restraint and stress. Working *with* a cooperative rather than *against* a resisting monkey (a) eliminates the handler's risk of becoming the target of defensive biting and scratching; (b) refines research methodology by controlling the extraneous variable of stress; and (c) provides high quality mental stimulation both to the animal and to the handling person. The initial time investment in the training quickly pays off in a safe handling procedure that no longer requires a second person to control the resisting subject.

It should be noted that the idea of training macaques to cooperate during blood collection is not new. There are reports from 10 different research facilities where macaques have been trained voluntarily to present a leg for blood collection (Reinhardt, 1997). Surprisingly, however, this simple, yet effective, refinement technique is applied only sporadically while the traditional technique relying on force still is prevailing.

ACKNOWLEDGMENT

This project was partly supported by NIH Grant RR–00167 to the Wisconsin Regional Primate Research Center.

REFERENCES

Ackerley, E. T., & Stones, P. B. (1969). Safety procedures for handling monkeys. *Laboratory Animal Handbooks, 4*, 207–211.
Albrecht, E. D., Nightingale, M. S., & Townsley, J. D. (1978). Stress-induced decrease in the serum concentration of progesterone in the pregnant baboon. *Journal of Endocrinology, 77*, 425–426.
Berendt, R., & Williams, T. D. (1971). The effect of restraint and position upon selected respiratory parameters of two species of *Macaca. Laboratory Animal Science, 21*, 502–509.
Brockway, B. P., Hassler, C. R., & Hicks, N. (1993). Minimizing stress during physiological monitoring. In S. M. Niemi, & J. E. Willson (Eds.), *Refinement and reduction in animal testing* (pp. 56–69) Bethesda, MD: Scientists Center for Animal Welfare.

Bush, M., Custer, R., Smeller, J., & Bush, L. M. (1977). Physiologic measures of nonhuman primates during physical restraint and chemical immobilization. *Journal of the American Veterinary Medicine Association, 171*, 866–869.

Cope, F. W., & Polis, B. D. (1959). Increased plasma glutamic-oxalacetic transaminase activity in monkeys due to nonspecific stress effect. *Journal of Aviation Medicine, 30*, 90–94.

Dettmer, E. L., Phillips, K. A., Rager, D. R., Bernstein, I., & Fragaszy, D. M. (1996). Behavioral and cortisol responses to repeated capture and venipuncture in *Cebus apella*. *American Journal of Primatology, 38*, 357–362.

Elvidge, H., Challis, J. R. G., Robinson, J. S., Roper, C., & Thorburn, G. D. (1976). Influence of handling and sedation on plasma cortisol in rhesus monkeys *(Macaca mulatta)*. *Journal of Endocrinology, 70*, 325–326.

Fuller, G. B., Hobson, W. C., Reyes, F. I., Winter, J. S. D., & Faiman, C. (1984). Influence of restraint and ketamine anesthesia on adrenal steroids, progesterone, and gonadotropins in rhesus monkeys. *Proceedings of the Society for Experimental Biology and Medicine, 175*, 487–490.

Golub, M. S., & Anderson, J. H. (1986). Adaptation of pregnant rhesus monkeys to short-term chair restraint. *Laboratory Animal Science, 36*, 507–511.

Goncharov, N. P., Taranov, A. G., Antonichev, A. V., Gorlushkin, V. M., Aso, T., Ckan, S. Z., et al. (1979). Effects of stress on the profile of plasma steroids in baboons *(Papio hamadryas)*. *Acta Endocrinologica, 90*, 372–384.

Goosen, D. J., Davies, J. H., Maree, M., & Dormehl, I. C. (1984). The influence of physical and chemical restraint on the physiology of the chacma baboon *(Papio ursinus)*. *Journal of Medical Primatology, 13*, 339–351.

Hayashi, K. T., & Moberg, G. P. (1987). Influence of acute stress and the adrenal axis on regulation of LH and testosterone in the male rhesus monkey *(Macaca mulatta)*. *American Journal of Primatology, 12*, 263–273.

Ives, M., & Dack, G. M. (1956). "Alarm reaction" and normal blood picture in *Macaca mulatta*. *Journal of Laboratory Clinical Medicine, 47*, 723–729.

Landi, M. S., Kissinger, J. T., Campbell, S. A., Kenney, C. A., & Jenkins, E. L. (1990). The effects of four types of restraint on serum alanine aminotransferase and asparate aminotransferase in the *Macaca fascicularis*. *Journal of the American College of Toxicology, 9*, 517–523.

Line, S. W., Markowitz, H., Morgan, K. N., & Strong, S. (1991). Effect of cage size and environmental enrichment on behavioral and physiological responses of rhesus macaques to the stress of daily events. In M. A. Novak & A. J. Petto (Eds.), *Through the looking glass: Issues of psychological well-being in captive nonhuman primates* (pp. 160–179) Washington, DC: American Psychological Association.

Loomis, M. R., Henrickson, R. V., & Anderson, J. H. (1980). Effects of ketamine hydrochloride on the hemogram of rhesus monkeys *(Macaca mulatta)*. *Laboratory Animal Science, 30*, 851–853.

Manning, P. J., Lehner, N. D. M., Feldner, M. A., & Bullock, B. C. (1969). Selected hematologic, serum chemical, and arterial blood gas characteristics of squirrel monkeys *(Saimiri sciureus)*. *Laboratory Animal Care, 19*, 831–837.

Mason, J. W., Wool, M. S., Wherry, F. E., Pennington, L. L., Brady, J. V., & Beer, B. (1968). Plasma growth hormone response to avoidance in the monkey. *Psychosomatic Medicine, 30*, 760–773.

Myers, B. A., Mendoza, S. P., & Cornelius, C. E. (1988). Elevation of plasma glucagon levels in response to stress in squirrel monkeys: Comparison of two subspecies *(Saimiri sciureus boliviensis* and *Saimiri sciureus sciureus)*. *Journal of Medical Primatology, 17*, 205–214.

Puri, C. P., Puri, V., & Anand-Kumar, T. C. (1981). Serum levels of testosterone, cortisol, prolactin and bioactive luteinizing hormone in adult male rhesus monkeys following cage-restraint or anaesthetizing with ketamine hydrochloride. *Acta Endocrinologica, 97*, 118–124.

Quadri, S. K., Pierson, C., & Spies, H. P. (1978). Effects of centrally acting drugs on serum levels in rhesus monkeys. *Neuroendocrinology, 27*, 136–147.

Reinhardt, V. (1991). Training adult male rhesus monkeys to actively cooperate during in-homecage venipuncture. *Animal Technology, 42,* 11–17.

Reinhardt, V. (1997). Training nonhuman primates to cooperate during blood collection: A review. *Laboratory Primate Newsletter, 36*(4), 1–4.

Reinhardt, V., & Cowley, D. (1992). In-homecage blood collection from conscious stumptailed macaques. *Animal Welfare, 1,* 249–255.

Reinhardt, V., & Reinhardt, A. (2000). Blood collection procedure of laboratory primates: A neglected variable in biomedical research. *Journal of Applied Animal Welfare Science, 3,* 321–333.

Robbins, D. Q., Zwick, H., Leedy, M., & Stearns, G. (1986). Acute restraint device for rhesus monkeys. *Laboratory Animal Science, 36,* 68–70.

Schnell, C. R., & Wood, J. M. (1993). Measurement of blood pressure, heart rate, body temperature, ECG and activity by telemetry in conscious unrestrained marmosets. *Proceedings of the Fifth Federation of European Laboratory Animal Science Associations Symposium,* 107–111.

Scientists Center for Animal Welfare. (1987). Consensus recommendations on effective institutional animal care and use committees. *Laboratory Animal Science, 37,* 11–13.

Streett, J. W., & Jonas, A. M. (1982). Differential effects of chemical and physical restraint on carbohydrate tolerance testing in nonhuman primates. *Laboratory Animal Science, 32,* 263–266.

Todd, H. E., Shideler, S. E., Laughlin, L. S., Overstreet, J. W., Pohl, C. R., Byrd, W., et al. (1999). Application of an enzyme immunoassay for urinary follicle-stimulating hormone to describe the effects of an acute stressor at different stages of the menstrual cycle in female laboratory macaques. *American Journal of Primatology, 48,* 135–151.

Torii, R., Kitagawa, N., Nigi, H., & Ohsawa, N. (1993). Effects of repeated restraint stress at 30-minute intervals during 24-hours on serum testosterone, LH and glucocorticoids levels in male Japanese monkeys (*Macaca fuscata*). *Experimental Animal, 42,* 67–73.

Valerio, D. A., Miller, R. L., Innes, J. R. M., Courntey, K. D., Pallotta, A. J., & Guttmacher, R. M. (1969). *Macaca mulatta: Management of a laboratory breeding colony.* New York: Academic.

Vertein, R., & Reinhardt, V. (1989). Training female rhesus monkeys to cooperate during in-homecage venipuncture. *Laboratory Primate Newsletter, 28*(2), 1–3.

Yasuda, M., Wolff, J., & Howard, C. F. (1988). Effects of physical and chemical restraint on intravenous glucose tolerance test in crested black macaques (*Macaca nigra*). *American Journal of Primatology, 15,* 171–180.

Zakaria, M., Lerche, N. W., Chomel, B. B., & Kass, P. H. (1996). Accidental injuries associated with nonhuman primate exposure at two Regional Primate Research Centers (U.S.A.): 1988–1993. *Laboratory Animal Science, 46,* 298–304.

JOURNAL OF APPLIED ANIMAL WELFARE SCIENCE, 6(3), 199–207
Copyright © 2003, Lawrence Erlbaum Associates, Inc.

Training Nonhuman Primates to Cooperate With Scientific Procedures in Applied Biomedical Research

Leah Scott, Peter Pearce, Sarah Fairhall, Neil Muggleton, and Jeremy Smith

Biomedical Sciences
Dstl Porton Down
Salisbury, Wiltshire, England

This report provides a brief overview of aspects of training nonhuman primates who have been, and continue to be, used in this laboratory. The research context involves applied behavioral studies in which animals are trained to perform complex operant behavioral sequences, often in their homecage environment. In such studies, animals have freedom to choose whether to engage in appetitively reinforced behavioral tests that employ neither food deprivation nor fluid management. This background of operant conditioning has provided an insight to, and a context for, animal training both as an adjunct to general laboratory management and as a way to expedite scientific procedures. Thus, training has potential implications for both well-being and scientific quality, although it must be considered an adjunct to the provision of socialization with conspecifics in high quality diverse housing systems and not as an alternative to such provision. The importance of discussion and consideration of alternative procedures cannot be overemphasized.

This article describes practical experience gained over more than 20 years in the training of nonhuman primates to cooperate with scientific procedures in an applied biomedical research setting. A number of techniques and approaches will be described that exemplify the culture in which the work is conducted.

The work of this laboratory has involved applied research in behavioral pharmacology and toxicology. The provision of high quality, healthy animals from in house colonies of marmosets (*Callithrix jacchus*) and rhesus monkeys (*Macaca*

Request for reprints should be sent to Leah Scott, Biomedical Sciences, Dstl Porton Down, Salisbury, Wiltshire, SP4 OJQ, England. E-mail: lascott@dstl.gov.uk

mulatta) has underpinned all the work. The opportunity to observe animals in breeding and peer groups has influenced staff attitudes and approaches positively to the care and use of the animals.

The nature of the applied research objectives has necessitated the development and application of measures of both spontaneous and conditioned behavior. This has provided opportunities to develop and validate a diverse range of novel experimental techniques for characterizing the common marmoset as a model in biomedical research and refining the use of rhesus monkeys in behavioral and pharmacological research. A cornerstone of the approach adopted has been the interrelationship between good welfare and scientific quality; the work is considered as a joint venture involving scientists, animal care staff, and the animals themselves.

METHODS

Rationale for Homecage Testing

Presentation of behavioral tests to nonhuman primates traditionally involves removing animals from their own cages and testing them in a remote location such as an operant chamber. In this laboratory, the emphasis on homecage testing exemplifies the culture that has been engendered, and this has provided a robust basis for training animals to cooperate with scientific procedures. The major feature of such testing is that although at times short-term separation from cage mates is necessary, such separation is undertaken within the confines of an extremely familiar environment, which would be expected to lead to significantly less stress in all concerned. Preliminary unpublished results in this laboratory suggest that short-term separation from a cage mate in an unfamiliar environment raises marmoset heart rate (as measured by radiotelemetry techniques) by about 30% compared to separation with visual contact within their cage environs.

Being unrestrained, animals are free to choose whether to engage in any task presented. Successful completion of conditioned tasks generally is associated with an opportunity to access preferred food treats, which normally are not incorporated in their regular diet. In such circumstances, no food or water deprivation is employed; negative reinforcement is never used. If animals choose not to engage in the task, they are free to move elsewhere in their enclosure.

Furthermore, homecage testing provides substantial levels of stimulation for all the animals in the room. This stimulation applies not only for the animal under test, as demonstrated by their willingness to participate, but also to others in the room who attend to the activities going on. They are able to do so because of the cage extensions, which allow observation of the whole room. It recently has been demonstrated, by means of 24-hr activity monitoring, that husbandry practices and the room activities associated with homecage testing have an impact on daily time budgets for marmosets—although it would be unwise to speculate about the desirability of such changes.

Development of the Approach

Traditional approaches to operant conditioning involve isolation of the subject in a sound-attenuated, temperature, and humidity-controlled environment such as that shown in Figure 1. When such approaches were used in this laboratory more than 20 years ago, adequate levels of performance were achieved, but isolation-induced vocalization was common and marmosets took many months to attain satisfactory baselines of performance on relatively simple schedules.

In parallel studies at that time, there was a requirement to quantify visually guided reaching in marmosets, and a simple apparatus that readily could be attached to—and detached from—the homecage was developed. The success of this approach (D'Mello, Duffy, & Miles, 1985) established confidence in the utility of homecage testing approaches and formed the basis for the subsequent development of methods for measuring more sophisticated behavioral indexes, such as attentional set shifting in marmosets and rhesus monkeys in the homecage (Crofts, Muggleton, Pearce, Nutt, & Scott, 1999). Homecage presentation of tasks, wherever practicable, now is the preferred approach.

FIGURE 1   An example of a marmoset pressing a lever to obtain reward in an operant box of traditional design, which is remote from the homecage.

Training Marmosets

Our operant training approaches are exemplified by recent and continuing studies in marmosets (Pearce, Crofts, Muggleton, & Scott, 1998). Animals are trained to perform complex cognitive tasks by responding to icons presented on a touch sensitive screen, which is positioned such that the animals can access the test equipment from a rigid cage extension on their homecage. In keeping with all operant training, it is essential to ensure that animals are (a) strongly motivated by the reward to be offered and (b) that they are familiar with the auditory and visual cues associated with availability of that reward.

Marmosets first are trained to lick up to 0.1 ml of banana milkshake (which has been demonstrated to be a powerful reinforcer in this and other laboratories) from a licker spout within a 5-sec period in response to a 1-sec tone. This is presented every 8 sec and, following establishment of reliable contingent licking, animals are trained to touch a colored square icon that initially fills the whole screen. Touching the screen is followed by the tone to indicate that the reward is available. They are encouraged to touch the screen by placing pieces of mastic or colored stickers on the screen. Once individuals touch the screen reliably, the mastic or stickers are removed and the animals encouraged to touch the screen unprompted to obtain the reward (see Figure 2). The dimensions of the icon then are gradually reduced until it approximates the size of the stimuli to be used in discrimination studies (see Figure 3). In this laboratory, the training protocol is successful without human participation.

Training sessions generally last for 30 min. When animals have achieved a predetermined level of performance, subsequent testing sessions of varying task com-

FIGURE 2   Marmoset responding to icons presented on a touch sensitive screen—making the correct response is rewarded with access to banana milkshake. The animal is free to return to the main body of the homecage at any time.

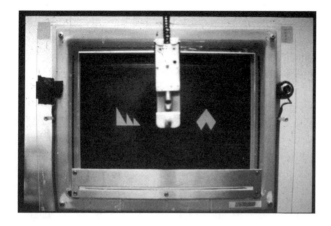

FIGURE 3   Examples of icons presented on the touchscreen with reward delivery device in the center.

plexity last for 15 min or terminate when 60 trials have been completed. It is important to note that the test, as presented, is self-paced. When the task increases in complexity, such as when the animal has to shift its attention from one icon type to another, fewer responses are made initially per test session because animals make more errors and choose to spend less time in close proximity to the touch screen.

The homecage testing approach is flexible in that a number of tasks can be presented sequentially, which maximizes the amount of information that can be collected from individual subjects. In an ongoing marmoset study, aspects of cognitive behavior and muscle function are investigated using different devices positioned on or near the cage front. Training for all testing procedures follows broadly similar patterns of successive approximation.

Leaving (and Returning to) the Homecage

It is not practicable to conduct all scientific procedures in the animal's homecage. Although it is possible to train some species to present limbs for blood sampling and drug administration, it sometimes is necessary to remove animals from their familiar environments for more complex procedures. When this is necessary, options for macaque species include the use of crushback cages or netting (in larger enclosures) with subsequent "manhandling." Neither option is ideal. Both can induce confrontation and high levels of stress for all concerned. Moreover, in many circumstances health and safety considerations dictate a "hands-off" approach. The preferred option for some studies in this laboratory has been to train animals to cooperate with pole and collar handling systems. Collars of an appropriate size and type do not appear to interfere with social behavior. Animals are readily trained to cooperate with attachment/detachment of a pole, and trained scientists/care staff direct the movement of animals toward the required destination.

In this laboratory, all rhesus monkeys (with or without collars) are trained to respond to voice commands. They are housed in large, interlinked cages with access to well equipped outdoor pens. When transfer to another location is required, knowledgeable, sympathetic staff use a consistent approach involving the animals' individual names and established methods of animal training (e.g., positive reinforcement, successive approximation) to encourage them to leave their home enclosure and enter another enclosure or transport box. To train animals to enter a transport box, which is attached to a door in the lower portion of the cage, they initially are separated into individual cages and the linkers closed. Early stages may involve positioning of staff above the level of the top of the cage; voice tones, which vary from one-word commands to softer reinforcement tones, are employed. Reducing the available space in the cage also may be used in the early stages. Once trained, animals will enter the transport box with little encouragement and generally following a single command. Grapes, which do not form part of the animals' regular diet, are used as a reward to reinforce this activity. As with other aspects of homecage testing, appropriately designed cages greatly facilitate the development and implementation of innovative techniques that are beneficial to animals, researchers, and animal care staff.

Eye Tracking

Studies of visual tracking are generally conducted in human and nonhuman primates. This is one of a number of areas of research that necessitate accurate positioning of the subject's head. When the subject is human, this does not present difficulties but traditional methods for nonhuman primates frequently involve highly invasive techniques and substantial restraint to restrict movement.

In some areas of work, when gaze orientation is under study and sophisticated neurophysiological recordings are not necessary, it is practicable to develop systems that do not necessitate substantial levels of restraint. Procedures involving voluntary cooperation can be devised, and this approach has been used successfully to track direction of gaze and pupil size in rhesus monkeys. To collect such information in humans, a commercially available system involving a pair of small cameras mounted on a headband (see Figure 4) has been employed. This arrangement would not be practicable for use with freely moving rhesus monkeys.

"Traditional" options would have involved the use of restraint chairs and the surgical implantation of scleral coils and head posts to limit head movement and facilitate measurement of gaze direction. Such techniques were not considered necessary in view of the nature of the study and the commitment of this laboratory

FIGURE 4   Human eye tracking system.

to using noninvasive or minimally invasive procedures wherever practicable. It was therefore decided to investigate options for a system based on cooperation.

Rhesus monkeys are trained to enter a specially modified transport box on voice command and then to place their heads through a hole in the roof to access a fruit-flavored drink, delivered via a specially designed ensemble that also defined the position of the subjects' eyes (Figure 5). This design is pivotal to the success of the approach. Subsequently, the animals are trained to respond by first fixing and then shifting their gaze in response to icons presented on a monitor screen. After a short test session of approximately 15 min (daily for 5 days per week), animals are returned to their cage mates. Throughout training and testing, animals are free to move within the constraints of the transport box and are not forced to engage with any the test procedures. For some areas of applied vision research, the technique may offer an alternative to more invasive methods.

CONCLUDING REMARKS AND RECOMMENDATIONS

This report gives a brief overview of aspects of training nonhuman primates that have been, and continue to be, used in this laboratory. The background of applied behavioral studies, in which animals are trained to perform complex behavioral sequences—often in their homecage environment—has provided an insight to, and a context for, animal training as an adjunct to general laboratory management and as a way to expedite scientific procedures.

A number of lessons have been learned over the years, and the concept of teaching the right lesson from the outset is a key element of all animal training—regardless of whether the training takes place in the homecage. The importance of this

FIGURE 5   A key element of the reward delivery ensemble; a molded device in the shape of an individual animal's face, which supports the fluid delivery tube.

concept was evident from homecage studies with rhesus monkeys in this laboratory 15 years ago.

There was a requirement to collect a precise measurement of reaction time, and the paradigm required a response key to be pressed until a signal light was illuminated. The animal then was required to release the response key as quickly as possible. All animals in the group, except one, learned the task very quickly, and their performances were consistent and predictable. When the animal who had not learned the task was filmed, it was clear that this animal was not performing the test properly. He was unable to detect illumination of the stimulus light because he was pressing the response key with his nose rather than his finger. The introduction of a small Perspex surround ensured that responses could be made only in the manner intended. This is an example of teaching the right lesson and of the value of observation, video recording, and appropriate evaluation.

Undoubtedly, there are benefits to be gained in terms of animal welfare and scientific quality, although these benefits will be optimized only if the prevailing culture of the laboratory is appropriate. At a very basic level, this involves striking an "appropriate" balance between human and nonhuman primate interactions. Furthermore, training and interactions with humans should be considered as adjuncts to the provision of socialization with conspecifics in high quality diverse housing systems and not as alternatives to such provision.

Communication on training issues is extremely important, whether by establishing personal contact, visiting facilities, sharing experiences in multidisciplinary forums, or publishing methodological details in mainstream physiological, behavioral, and applied scientific reports in specialist primatological and welfare journals. Publication of reports on unsuccessful techniques also is extremely useful as valuable lessons can be learned. Critical evaluation and widespread dissemination and discussion of relevant findings are extremely important issues.

There is a continuing requirement for creativity, lateral thinking, and open-mindedness to consider how aspects of techniques and approaches developed and implemented by other laboratories might be adapted and adopted to refine procedures. Spending time with individuals who have relevant practical experience can de-risk such ventures substantially and can pay real dividends in terms of animal welfare and scientific quality.

ACKNOWLEDGMENTS

We acknowledge the contributions of many who have been influential in their thinking and approaches—especially Viktor Reinhardt, Hal Markowitz, Joachim Jaekel, and Trevor Poole. We acknowledge the commitment over the years of many teams of scientists, animal care staff, and technical support staff at Dstl Porton Down, which has contributed to the culture in which animal training has been undertaken and continues to be fostered.

REFERENCES

Crofts, H. S., Muggleton, N. G., Pearce, P. C., Nutt, D. J., & Scott, E. A. M. (1999). Home cage presentation of complex discrimination tasks to marmosets and rhesus monkeys. *Laboratory Animals, 33,* 207–214.

D'Mello, G. D., Duffy, E. A., & Miles, S. S. (1985). A conveyor belt task for assessing visuo-motor coordination in the marmoset (*Callithrix jacchus*): Effects of diazepam, chlorpromazine, pentobarbital and d-amphetamine. *Psychopharmacology (Berl), 86,* 125–31.

Pearce, P. C., Crofts, H. S., Muggleton, N. G., & Scott, E. A. M. (1998). Concurrent monitoring of EEG and performance in the Common Marmoset (*Callithrix jacchus*): A methodological approach. *Physiology and Behaviour, 63,* 591–599.

JOURNAL OF APPLIED ANIMAL WELFARE SCIENCE, 6(3), 209–220
Copyright © 2003, Lawrence Erlbaum Associates, Inc.

Training Common Marmosets (*Callithrix jacchus*) to Cooperate During Routine Laboratory Procedures: Ease of Training and Time Investment

Jean McKinley, Hannah M. Buchanan-Smith,
and Lois Bassett
Department of Psychology
University of Stirling

Keith Morris
MRC Human Reproductive Sciences Unit
Edinburgh, Scotland

The first author trained 12 laboratory-housed common marmosets (*Callithrix jacchus*) in pairs to assess the practicality of positive reinforcement training as a technique in the management of these nonhuman animals. Behaviors taught were (a) target training to allow in homecage weighing and (b) providing urine samples. Between 2 to 13, 10-minute training sessions established desired behaviors. Training aggressive animals only after they had been fed eliminated aggression during training. Trained animals proved extremely reliable, and data collection using trained animals was considerably faster than collection using current laboratory techniques. The results suggest that positive reinforcement training is a practical option in the management of laboratory-housed marmosets.

A review of early research into the care of common marmosets (*Callithrix jacchus*) reveals just how much progress has been made in housing and feeding of these nonhuman animals (Epple, 1970; Hiddleston, 1978; Lunn & Hearn, 1978; Poole,

---

Requests for reprints should be sent to Hannah M. Buchanan-Smith, Scottish Primate Research Group, Department of Psychology, University of Stirling, Stirling FK9 4LA, Scotland. E-mail: h.m.buchanan-smith@stir.ac.uk

Hubrecht, & Kirkwood, 1999). However, these articles also reveal few changes in how marmosets are managed during routine laboratory procedures.

The current Home Office (1986) code of practice for the housing and care of animals used in scientific procedures states that, for primates, "The least distressing method of handling is to train the animal to cooperate in routine procedures" (Sec 3, para 50). However, the literature that shows that training both facilitates data collection and reduces stress in primates in the laboratory largely concerns the training of macaques (Reinhardt, 1997). The *Universities Federation for Animal Welfare (UFAW) Handbook* (Poole et al., 1999) stated that marmosets can be trained for routine husbandry and experimental procedures but does not provide details on how to train, or the cost effectiveness of the training versus alternative practices. Anzenberger and Gossweiler (1993) used the tendency of marmosets to urinate immediately on leaving the nestbox each morning to develop a technique allowing in-homecage collection of urine samples. However, although useful in some settings, this technique may not be practical with cage-housed animals because of the need for specially designed apparatus and overnight confinement in the nestbox. In addition, this method only allows collection of first void and therefore is unsuitable for frequent sampling throughout the day.

Despite its growing popularity in the management of macaques, training has not been widely adopted in the management of laboratory-housed marmosets. One reason may be that the need for improved methods has not yet been perceived. Motivation to encourage cooperation is greatly increased when handling potentially dangerous animals (Kiley-Worthington, 1990). Due to their small size, marmosets are easily handled, and a stout pair of gloves is all that is required to protect the handler from bites and scratches.

Although handling these monkeys poses few problems in terms of human safety, it is widely noted that this can cause considerable distress, not only for the animal but for others housed in the same area (National Research Council, 1998). In addition, both removal from the homecage (Norcross & Newman, 1999) and methods used for capture can be problematic. The use of nets can result in injury; thus, the recommended method is to trap these animals in their nestbox (National Research Council, 1998). However, Poole (1998) reported that a secure place to hide or rest is one of the fundamental psychological needs of mammals. As marmosets both sleep in these boxes and retreat there when threatened, there is a potential welfare problem in using nestboxes as a means of capture.

Positive reinforcement training (PRT) rewards an animal for performing a desired behavior. No coercion is used; mistakes are ignored, not punished, leaving the animal to choose whether he/she will participate in the training program (Pryor, 1999). An example of this technique is target training. Here, the animal is rewarded for holding a specific object whenever it is presented. This simple behavior then can be used in a variety of ways; moving animals between locations, entering transport cages, and keeping animals at specific locations. This technique has been used to improve husbandry and veterinary care, reduce abnormal behavior and aggression, and promote the safety of personnel (Laule, Bloomsmith, & Schapiro, 2003/this issue).

However, when alternative methods of handling are sought, there are a number of practical reasons why PRT may not be considered. Many laboratory animals are destined for terminal studies; thus, their time in the laboratory may be limited, decreasing the return on initial time investment. Although appropriate in a zoo setting with relatively few animals, training is not widely regarded as practical in a laboratory housing hundreds of individuals. Although the need to invest time during the training process cannot be denied, the possibility that this investment may be recouped through faster data collection often is not considered. This is an important issue as changes intended to promote welfare stand little chance of being widely implemented unless they can be shown to be practical. There also is a widespread belief that animals will cooperate for rewards only as a consequence of food or water deprivation. Kiley-Worthington (1990) suggested that such beliefs are a legacy of the era of "Skinner box" experiments on reinforcement, and a glance through any behaviorist textbook does reveal numerous studies on the behavior of hungry and thirsty rats (e.g., Pearce, 1997).

The aim of this study was to assess the practicality of PRT with common marmosets in a laboratory setting. Recording weights and collecting urine samples through the use of metabolism cages are noninvasive procedures but usually require capture and removal from the homecage, potentially causing distress (Norcross & Newman, 1999). To avoid this, animals were trained to allow in homecage data collection. Research questions were as follows:

1. Can common marmosets be trained using solely positive reinforcement techniques and, if so, how much time investment is required?
2. Will trained animals cooperate reliably enough to allow regular data collection?
3. How does data collection using trained animals compare to those using current practices with regard to time required for each technique?

METHODS

Study Animals

The study animals were 6 male and 6 female common marmosets housed in pairs, with a mean age 1,188 days ($\pm$ SE 232.37 days). Initial criteria for selection was that at least one member of each pair would take a food reward from the trainer's hand. Pairs who showed aggression at this stage were not selected.

Although the standard practice at the unit was to refer to marmosets by identity number, all study animals were named prior to training. (See Table 1).

Housing and Husbandry

The marmosets were housed in male/female pairs in the same colony room at the Medical Research Council (MRC) Human Reproductive Sciences Unit, Edinburgh, Scotland. This room measured 2.7m × 3m × 5m and contained eight housing units, each subdivided into four sections measuring 55cm wide × 95cm high × 110cm deep, with one pair per section. Of the study animals, three pairs were housed in upper tier cages, and three pairs were housed in the lower tier. Cages had wood shavings as a floor substrate and were furnished with a nestbox, shelves, and two wooden logs. Some cages contained additional enrichment devices. Water was available *ad libitum* from a bottle mounted on the front mesh of the cage. Rooms were maintained at a temperature of 22 to 24°C and a relative humidity of 50%.

Food was provided once a day at about 1230h. The marmosets were fed with commercially manufactured primate pellets (Mazuri Primate Diet, E; Witham, Essex, England) and a variety of fresh fruit (banana, apple, pear, orange, tomato and grapes). This was supplemented by either a high protein porridge or a mixture of dried fruit and nuts. Of the food items available, the primate pellets were the least preferred and the most likely to be removed uneaten during morning cage cleaning. To encourage their consumption, the proportion of fresh fruit in the diet was reduced over weekends.

TABLE 1
Details of Study Animals

Pair	Name	Sex	Age at Start of Study	Relationship
1	Cecil	M	2 years 4 months	Siblings
	Coco	F	1 year 11 months	
2	Freddy	M	2 years 6 months	Siblings
	Foxy	F	2 years 6 months	
3	Iggy	M	2 years 6 months	None
	Iris	F	3 years 6 months	
4	Jambo	M	6 years 7 months	Father/daughter
	Jilly	F	1 year 6 months	
5	Kipper	M	1 year 6 months	Siblings
	Keltie	F	1 year 11 months	
6	Leo	M	2 years 8 months	None
	Lala	F	2 years 6 months	

Procedure

Of the study animals, Pairs 1, 2, and 3 were target trained first and then trained to urinate. The remaining three pairs (Pairs 4, 5, and 6) had the order of training reversed. When members of a pair learned the desired behavior at different rates, the trained animal was rewarded only when the behavior followed the verbal cue "go on" (i.e., spontaneous responses were no longer reinforced). These animals were asked to perform at intervals throughout each training session, thus maintaining their behavior while allowing the training of their partner to continue.

Three different food rewards were used. These, in order of preference, were small pieces of marshmallow, cornflakes, and chopped dates. Attempts were made to avoid the use of sweet items and use healthier rewards. Perhaps due to the varied diet the study animals received, these attempts proved unsuccessful. If any animal showed aggressive behavior toward a partner, training was terminated immediately, and a lower value food reward was used during the next session.

Reliability of Trained Animals

Reliability of the trained animals was assessed by recording weights and collecting urine for cortisol analysis (Bassett, Buchanan-Smith, McKinley, & Smith, 2003/this issue) and by calculating the percentage of required weights and urine samples obtained.

Target Training for in Homecage Weighing

Each training session lasted a maximum of 10 min, ending sooner if each animal had earned 12 rewards. When an animal held the target for 20 sec, the scales were introduced. Animals were considered trained when they remained on the scales long enough to allow their weight to be noted. A shaping procedure was used with training progressing in stages:

1. The target (a plastic spoon) was held at the front of the cage with the food reward held behind it. Males were offered a black target placed on the left-hand side and females a white target placed on the right. Initially the target was touched as the marmoset reached for the food. A reward was given when the correct target was touched. Incorrect responses were ignored.

2. The target was presented without the reward held behind it. Marmosets were rewarded when target touched.

3. The time the target had to be held before reward was given was gradually increased (see Figure 1).

FIGURE 1   Target trained female holds her target as male is given his.

FIGURE 2   Weighing: Female sits on scales as male waits until his target is presented.

4. Scales for weighing were placed in the cage and the target held in front of them. The marmoset was rewarded for climbing onto the scales and holding the target (see Figure 2).

Urine Training

Marmosets were rarely observed urinating but scent marked frequently, depositing a few drops of urine each time. Scent marking is a behavior that occurs fairly frequently in common marmosets (Epple, 1970; Stevenson & Poole, 1976) and, as observed by H. M. Buchanan-Smith, in this population in particular. It proved more practical to reinforce this behavior than to wait for urination. The criterion for success of urine training was that each animal scent marked on request 12 times per 10-min session.

As previously described, a shaping procedure was used with training progressing in stages. To allow immediate reinforcement of desired behaviors, a clicking sound was used as a bridging stimulus. Commercially available "clickers" proved too loud and startled the marmosets; therefore, the trainer (J. McKinley) created the sound by clicking her tongue. Five stages were employed during training:

1. The marmosets were taught to associate tongue clicking with a food reward (i.e., the trainer clicked her tongue and then rewarded both pair members). The association was considered formed when the marmosets moved rapidly to the front of the cages and reached for food as soon as the clicking sound was made.

2. Each pair in turn was observed by the trainer who waited for scent marking to occur spontaneously. Whenever a marmoset scent marked a branch, the trainer made a clicking noise and rewarded that animal.

3. When the rate of scent marking had increased, a verbal request was given as the animal moved toward the sites where scent marking occurred. An animal who then scent marked was rewarded.

4. Once the marmoset scent marked on verbal request, rewards were given only for marking one or two specific sites.

5. Holes were drilled at sites used by the marmosets to allow insertion of collecting vials.

Comparing Data Collection Using Trained Animals and Standard Laboratory Procedures

Weighing.   The time taken to record the weights of the trained animals was compared to that taken using the current standard procedure. Data were collected when the study animals were weighed during another study (Bassett et al., 2003/this issue). Timing began when the cage door was opened. The monkeys were confined in their nestbox and then taken to the procedure room. Each, in turn, was removed and placed in a weighing cage, weighed, and then returned to the nestbox. Timing ended when cage door was closed after the monkeys were returned to their homecage. For the trained marmosets, timing began when the cage door was opened to allow insertion of the scales and ended when the door was closed after removal.

Urine versus blood sampling.   Urine is not collected routinely in this laboratory. Therefore, time taken to collect urine samples was compared to that taken to collect blood samples, as many tests conducted on blood also can be carried out using urine. Data were collected during routine blood draws. The standard practice is to collect all animals due to have samples taken simultaneously. This is done by confining them in their nestboxes and transporting them to the procedures room. When all samples are collected, the animals are returned to their homecage. Timing began when the first cage door was opened and ended when the last animal was returned to the homecage. For urine sampling, timing began when first cage door was opened to allow insertion of the first collecting vial and ended when the last sample was removed and the door closed. In all cases, time recorded was divided by the number of samples obtained to give an estimate of time taken per sample.

RESULTS

Reliability

After training, during formal data collection, the trained animals proved extremely reliable with 100% of weights ($n = 12$) and 95% of required urine samples being successfully collected ($n = 312$).

Time Investment in Training

There was considerable variation in the speed with which each animal learned to perform the tasks. The time required to complete target training ranged from 2 to 12 sessions (20 min to 2 hr overall, $M = 1$ hr, 4 min, per pair), whereas urine training was accomplished in 3 to 13 sessions (30 min to 2 hr, 10min, $M = 52$ min, per pair). There was no difference by sex for either target training, $t(10) = 0.22$, $p = .83$, or urine training, $t(10) = 0.47$, $p = .65$. Figure 3 shows the number of sessions required for individual animals.

When the marmosets were grouped according to which behavior was learned first, animals who were urine trained first learned significantly faster than those who were target trained first, $F(1, 10) = 157$, $p < .001$. When urine training was conducted first, this behavior was established within a mean of 4.5 sessions (around 45 min, per pair). Target training was accomplished within two sessions (20 min, per pair). Figure 4 shows the mean number of sessions required per individual for both trained behaviors depending on training order.

Comparison Between Trained Animals and Routine Laboratory Procedures

When the time taken to record the weights of the trained animals was compared to weights recorded by the current standard procedure, data collection from

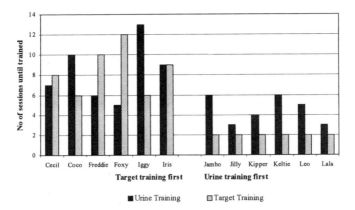

FIGURE 3   Number of training sessions required by each study animal to reach training criterion.

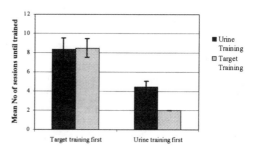

FIGURE 4   Mean number of sessions required for each behavior to reach training criterion by training order (bars show standard errors).

trained animals was considerably faster (see Table 2). Time taken per urine sample was less than that typically taken to collect blood samples.

DISCUSSION

This study demonstrated that training marmosets to cooperate with routine laboratory procedures could be accomplished using only PRT. One problem initially encountered while training pairs was four instances of aggression when the dominant animal tried to steal the reward. All of these incidences of aggression occurred when the monkeys were hungry (e.g., before they were fed), with three occurring on a Monday (after 2 days when the proportion of fresh fruit in the diet was reduced). Aggression was eliminated by training pairs with an aggressive member only after they had been fed and rewarding responses with cornflakes rather than marshmallow at the start of each session. Cornflakes are a less preferred food and were usually accepted three or four times and then discarded. Monday morning sessions were discontinued. These findings on aggres-

TABLE 2
Mean Time Required Per Sample Collected Using Trained Animals
Compared With Standard Laboratory Procedures

Procedure	Mean Time Per Sample[a]
Weighing (standard procedure)	174.25
Weighing (trained animals)	14.75
Blood sample collection	542.8
Urine sample collection	184.6

[a]Given in seconds.

sion have far-reaching implications. They counter the widely held belief that food deprivation is necessary for successful training. Indeed, they even suggest that food deprivation may be counterproductive to the training process.

Weights were collected with 100% reliability. Around 5% of urine samples were lost, largely due to the same animal, not because he failed to provide a sample, but because he became adept at removing the collecting vial before the trainer. In a comparison of urine versus blood collection, it should be noted that it could be difficult to collect daily blood samples over a long period of time without damage to the femoral vein. In addition, there is a limit to how much blood can be taken from such a small animal before his or her health is compromised (Ferrell, 2003; Hearn, 1983). Training to provide urine samples could be particularly useful for studies of relatively long duration. However, as scent marking is associated with stress in marmosets (Bassett et al., 2003/this issue), there is the issue of rewarding a stress-related behavior (Sutcliffe & Poole, 1978; Watson, Ward, Davis, & Stavisky, 1999). However, the study animals did not continue to scent mark at high rates outside training sessions despite this behavior having been rewarded (Bassett et al., 2003/this issue). Many substances such as cortisol can now be measured in saliva (Lutz, Tiefenbacher, Jorgensen, Meyer, & Novak, 2000), and this may prove a more satisfactory replacement for blood and urine. Saliva can be collected at very regular intervals (i.e., 5 min), and training is minimal.

Although the marmosets learned both behaviors fairly quickly, there was considerable variation in the speed with which individual marmosets learned; it would seem that overcoming fear of humans was an important factor in their performance. Initially the marmosets were nervous and tended to take the food reward, then retreat to the back of the cage before eating. They only would remain holding their targets once this nervousness had been overcome during the training process. Some primates scent marked more frequently when nervous (Watson et al., 1999), and this did appear to be the case with these animals. Initial nervousness, although a hindrance during target training, was actually helpful during urine training, as frequent scent marking allowed frequent reinforcement of this behavior. By the time urine training was complete, the marmosets had become quite tame, and this made target training easier.

A positive consequence of PRT is that the caregiver–animal relationship is richer. Although this clearly has benefits for animal welfare, it has a potentially negative side effect. Personnel involved in terminal studies frequently maintain a degree of psychological detachment through avoidance of naming or anything else that might personify the study animals (Serpell, 1999). PRT could make detachment from the animal as a means of coping with euthanasia more difficult.

Once training was complete, data collection for trained animals was considerably faster than that collected using standard procedures, suggesting that time invested in training may be recouped later. In this study, time spent target training for weighing could be recovered within 8 to 20 sessions, depending on training order. However, as the marmosets were trained in pairs, with two sessions being conducted simultaneously, the number of sessions required per animal actually overestimates the actual time investment required. The basic behavior is extremely versatile and, once established, could be used for other procedures such as entering transport cages (Laule & Desmond, 1998). We conclude that training is a practical tool in the management of these animals and allows them to cope better with routine laboratory procedures (Bassett et al., 2003/this issue).

ACKNOWLEDGMENTS

The Carnegie Trust for the Universities of Scotland and the Faculty for Human Sciences, University of Stirling funded this research, and we are grateful for their support. We would like to thank the staff at the MRC Human Reproductive Sciences Unit for their help during this study and Mark Prescott for helpful comments on the manuscript.

REFERENCES

Anzenberger, G., & Gossweiler, H. (1993). How to obtain individual urine samples from undisturbed marmoset families. *American Journal of Primatology, 31,* 223–230.

Bassett, L., Buchanan-Smith, H. M., McKinley, J., & Smith, T. E. (2003/this issue). Effects of training on stress-related behavior of the common marmoset (*Callithrix jacchus*) in relation to coping with routine husbandry procedures. *Journal of Applied Animal Welfare Science, 6,* 221–233.

Epple, G. (1970). Maintenance, breeding, and development of marmoset monkeys (*Callitricidae*) in captivity. *Folia Primatologica, 12,* 56–76.

Ferrell, T. (2003). Limits on blood drawing. *Laboratory Primate Newsletter, 42,* 4–5.

Hearn, J. P. (1983). The common marmoset (Callithrix jacchus). In J. Hearn (Ed.), *Reproduction in the New World primates: New models in medical research* (pp. 181–215). Lancaster, England: MTP.

Hiddleston, W. A. (1978). The production of the common marmoset (*Callithrix jacchus*) as a laboratory animal. In D. J. Chivers & W. Lane-Petter (Eds.), *Recent advances in primatology* (pp. 173–181). London: Academic.

Home Office. (1986). *Code of practice for the housing and care of animals in designated breeding and supply establishments*. London: Her Majesty's Stationery Office.

Kiley-Worthington, M. (1990). *Animals in circuses and zoos: Chiron's world?* Essex, England: Little Eco-Farms.

Laule, G. E., Bloomsmith, M. A., & Schapiro, S. J. (2003/this issue). The use of positive reinforcement training techniques to enhance the care, management, and welfare of laboratory primates. *Journal of Applied Animal Welfare Science, 6,* 163–173.

Laule, G., & Desmond, T. (1998). Positive reinforcement training as an enrichment strategy. In D. J. Shepherdson, J. D. Mellon, & M. Hutchins (Eds.), *Second nature: Environmental enrichment for captive animals* (pp. 302–313). London: Smithsonian Institution Press.

Lunn, S. F., & Hearn, J. P. (1978). Breeding marmosets for medical research. In D. J. Chivers, & W. Lane-Petter (Eds.), *Recent advances in primatology* (pp. 183–185). London: Academic.

Lutz, C. K., Tiefenbacher, S., Jorgensen, M. J., Meyer, J. S., & Novak, M. A. (2000). Techniques for collecting saliva from awake, unrestrained, adult monkeys for cortisol assay. *American Journal of Primatology, 52,* 93–99.

National Research Council. (1998). *The psychological well-being of nonhuman primates*. Washington, DC: National Academy Press.

Norcross, J. L., & Newman, J. D. (1999). Effects of separation and novelty on distress vocalisations and cortisol in the common marmoset (*Callithrix jacchus*). *American Journal of Primatology, 47,* 209–222.

Pearce, J. M. (1997). *Animal learning and conditioning: An introduction*. Hove, England: Psychology Press.

Poole, T. B. (1998). Meeting a mammal's psychological needs: Basic principles. In D. J. Shepherdson, J. D. Mellon, & M. Hutchins (Eds.), *Second nature: Environmental enrichment for captive animals*. (pp. 83–94). London: Smithsonian Institution Press.

Poole, T., Hubrecht, R., & Kirkwood, J. K. (1999). Marmosets and tamarins. In T. Poole (Ed.). *UFAW handbook on the care and management of laboratory animals, 7th edition. Volume 1—Terrestrial vertebrates* (pp. 559–573). Oxford, England: Blackwell Science.

Pryor, K. (1999). *Don't shoot the dog: The new art of teaching and training*. New York: Bantam.

Reinhardt, V. (1997). Training nonhuman primates to cooperate during blood collection: A review. *Laboratory Primate Newsletter, 36*(4), 1–4.

Serpell, J. A. (1999). Sheep in wolves' clothing? Attitudes to animals among farmers and scientists. In F. L. Dolins (Ed.), *Attitudes to animals: Views in animal welfare* (pp. 26–33). Cambridge, England: Cambridge University Press.

Stevenson, M. F., & Poole, T. B. (1976). An ethogram of the common marmoset *(Callithrix jacchus jacchus)*: General behavioural repertoire. *Animal Behaviour, 24,* 428–451.

Sutcliffe, A. G., & Poole, T. B. (1978). Scent marking and associated behaviour in captive common marmosets (*Callithrix jacchus jacchus*) with a description of the histology of scent glands. *Journal of Zoology, London, 185,* 41–56.

Watson, S. L., Ward, J. P., Davis, K. B, & Stavisky, R. C. (1999). Scent-marking and cortisol response in the small-eared bushbaby (*Otolemur garettii*). *Physiology and Behavior, 66,* 695–699.

JOURNAL OF APPLIED ANIMAL WELFARE SCIENCE, 6(3), 221–233
Copyright © 2003, Lawrence Erlbaum Associates, Inc.

Effects of Training on Stress-Related Behavior of the Common Marmoset (*Callithrix jacchus*) in Relation to Coping With Routine Husbandry Procedures

Lois Bassett, Hannah M. Buchanan-Smith, and Jean McKinley

Department of Psychology
University of Stirling

Tessa E. Smith

Department of Biological Sciences
Chester College of Higher Education

Using positive reinforcement, J. McKinley trained 12 common marmosets *(Callithrix jacchus)* to provide urine samples on request. The study then exposed the marmosets to mildly stressful, routine husbandry procedures (i.e., capture and weighing). The nonhuman animals spent less time inactive poststressor as opposed to prestressor. L. Bassett collected matched behavioral data from 12 nontrained marmosets who were less accustomed to human interaction. These animals spent significantly more time self-scratching and locomoting as well as less time inactive, poststressor. Collapsed data from the 2 populations showed increased scent marking, poststressor. These results suggest that locomotion, self-scratching, and scent marking are useful, noninvasive behavioral measures of stress and, thus, reduced welfare in the common marmoset. Overall, nontrained animals showed more self-scratching than did their trained counterparts. It was not possible to collect urine from nontrained marmosets. In response to the stressor, however, trained animals showed no significant change in excreted urinary cortisol. These results suggest that training marmosets may allow them to cope better with routine laboratory procedures.

Requests for reprints should be sent to Hannah M. Buchanan-Smith, Department of Psychology, University of Stirling, Stirling, FK9 4LA, Scotland. E-mail: h.m.buchanan-smith@stir.ac.uk

The common marmoset (*Callithrix jacchus*) is used extensively in behavioral (Williams, 1987) and biomedical (Hearn, Abbott, Chalmers, Hodges, & Lunn, 1978) research. Despite this, there has been a paucity of studies attempting to identify behaviors associated with increased or decreased welfare, resulting from the captive environment, husbandry procedures, or experimental manipulations. Johnson et al. (1996) found an increase in plasma cortisol in this species, in response to isolation, to be associated with increased movement, which was interpreted as an indicator of behavioral arousal. In contrast, increases in plasma cortisol because of housing in an unstable peer group were associated with increases in aggressive and submissive behaviors related to agonistic encounters.

Orally administered anxiety-reducing benzodiazepine drugs have been shown to reduce the frequency of self-scratching in the common marmoset (Cilia & Piper, 1997), suggesting that this behavior may be associated with stress. In the same study, the anxiolytic drugs resulted in decreases in scent marking and aggressive behavior. Increases in allogrooming also were seen following drug administration, indicating that muscle relaxation was not responsible for the decreases in the other behaviors seen. Anxiolytic drugs did not, however, affect rates of locomotion. This suggests, in contrast to the study by Johnson et al. (1996), that locomotory behavior is unrelated to anxiety.

Increased activity in the hypothalamic-pituitary-adrenal (HPA) axis in response to physical or psychological challenge results in elevated circulatory glucocorticoids such as cortisol. Various species of primates show increases in plasma cortisol in response to stressors such as restraint (Reinhardt, Liss, & Stevens, 1995), exposure to high intensity noise (Hanson, Larson, & Snowdon, 1976), and maternal separation (Hennessy, 1997). Studies also have assayed urine for cortisol concentrations (Crockett, 1998). Use of urine or saliva as opposed to blood has the advantage in that it may be collected noninvasively. Blood collection procedures involving capture; restraint; and, possibly, anesthesia may, themselves, result in elevated cortisol levels, affecting experimental results. Weid's black, tufted-ear marmosets (*Callithrix kuhli*), trained to give urine samples on request, show significantly elevated levels of urinary cortisol following a stressor such as isolation in a small cage for 11 hr (Smith & French, 1997).

This study aimed to validate the use of both behavior and urinary cortisol as reliable and sensitive measures of stress and, therefore, welfare in the common marmoset. Both behavioral and physiological measures may be useful as welfare indicators (Duncan & Fraser, 1997; Mason & Mendl, 1993). A demonstrable positive or negative correlation between urinary cortisol concentration and frequency of a particular behavior following a stressor will increase the validity of the use of changes in frequency of the behavior as an effective indirect welfare indicator (Mason & Mendl, 1993). Prior experience of positive handling affects responses to stressors in many species of animal, and taming may reduce the physiological activity of the HPA axis (Grandin, 1997). Therefore, this study also sought to assess the effects of training in relation to welfare and coping with routine laboratory procedures.

METHOD

Study Animals

The study animals were 24 common marmosets—12 males and 12 females—with a mean age of 1,089 days (± SE 135.67) as of January 2, 2001. Animals in the training group (n = 12 animals) had a mean age of 1,188 days (± SE 232.37 days) and those in the nontraining group (n = 12 animals), a mean age of 989 days (± SE 145.55 days). The ages of animals in the two groups were not significantly different from each other, $t(12)$ = 0.72; p = .13.

The marmosets were housed in male–female pairs at the Medical Research Council (MRC) Human Reproductive Sciences Unit, Edinburgh, Scotland. See McKinley, Buchanan-Smith, Bassett, and Morris (2003/this issue) for details of housing. Animals in upper and lower tier cages were balanced between conditions. All trained marmosets were housed in cages within the same colony room, and nontrained animals in an adjacent room. None of the females in the study were past the first trimester of pregnancy, as detected by transabdominal uterine palpations, which were performed regularly. This generally is considered a reliable method for detecting pregnancy in this species (Hearn et al., 1978) and was important as cortisol levels may be affected by pregnancy (Bazer, 1998). Over a period of approximately 6 weeks, McKinley (McKinley et al., 2003/this issue) trained animals in the training group to provide urine samples for analysis. Animals in the nontraining group were not trained and were not exposed to any additional positive human interaction.

Experimental Procedure

On the day of the stressor, each of the animals was chased into the nestbox, which then was closed and removed from the cage. The nestbox was taken into a separate room in which the marmosets were removed one at a time and transferred by gloved hand to a small cage to be weighed. They then were returned to the nestbox, which was replaced in the homecage and opened to allow the animals to re-enter the homecage at will. The whole procedure took between 4 min and 4 min, 30 sec for trained animals (mean time 4 min, 9 sec; ± SE 4.73 sec) and 3 min, 45 sec and 4 min, 30 sec (mean time 4 min, 14 sec; ± SE 7.24 sec) for nontrained animals. The amount of time spent away from the homecage was not significantly different for animals in training and nontraining groups, $t(10)$ =

–0.578, p = .58. The stressors were administered on March 7, 2001 and March 14, 2001 (both Wednesdays) between 0930h and 1030h. Removal from the homecage for weighing is a standard laboratory procedure and is carried out several times a year.

Cortisol Enzyme Immunoassay

T. E. Smith (then of Queen's University, Belfast, Ireland) measured cortisol concentrations in all urine samples. The enzyme immunoassay was validated immunologically as described by Reimers, Salerno, and Lamb (1996). Serial dilutions of four urine pools gave parallel displacement curves with a standard solution. This confirmed that the cortisol in the urine samples was identical immunologically with standard cortisol preparations (from Sigma Chemical Company). Recovery of known amounts of cortisol standard (n = 5 stds: 500, 250, 125, 62.5, 31.25 pg/50ul) from high and low concentrations of a urine pool had a mean of 80.83 ± SE 1.9 (n = 3 repeats for high pool and 3 repeats for low pool). Intra-assay coefficients of variation for high and low concentration pools were 4.68% and 1.91%, respectively (n = 11). Inter-assay coefficients of variation for high and low concentration pools were 9.30% and 14.89%, respectively (n = 11). Sensitivity was 1.95 pg/50ul, equivalent to 39 pg/1ml. To correct for urine dilution, creatinine concentrations were quantified for each sample (Tietz, 1976) and cortisol expressed as μg cortisol/mg Cr/ml.

Behavioral Data Collection and Statistical Analysis

Urine was collected immediately after the behavioral data were recorded. Scan sampling was used with an interval of 15 sec between scans; data collection sessions lasted for 5 min. Data were collected on a palm top computer using The Observer 3.0 software (Noldus, 1993). The recorded behaviors were mutually exclusive and included "Inactive," "Locomote," "Self-Scratch," "Scent Mark," "Vocalize," and "Forage" (see Table 1).

An "other" category also was used and included behaviors infrequently seen, such as "allogrooming" and "inactive, inalert" behavior. One set of prestressor data was recorded for each monkey (trained and nontrained) at each of three time periods, 1200h, 1400h, and 1600h. Matching data were collected for both groups following administration of the stressor. No significant main effects were found for vocalizing or foraging; therefore, these data are not discussed further. Data were found to be normally distributed throughout; hence, parametric tests were used. A two-factor, within-subjects analysis of variance (ANOVA) was used to test for effect of stress condition (pre- and poststressor) and time of day (1200h, 1400h, and 1600h) on uri-

TABLE 1
Mutually Exclusive Behavioral Categories and Definitions Used for Common Marmosets

Behavioral Category	Definition
Inactive	Animal remains alert and in one location, without engaging in any other activity
Locomote	Animal moves between locations by walking, climbing, running, or jumping
Self-Scratch	Animal scratches itself with a hand or foot
Scent Mark[a]	Animal sits and rubs anogenital area on branch or other area of enclosure (anal scent mark), or rubs sternal area along substrate (sternal scent mark)
Vocalize	Animal emits any kind of vocalization audible to observer; animal must also be seen to vocalize for this behavior to be scored; this category takes priority over the other behaviors
Forage	Animal is engaged in any activity directly related to acquiring or ingesting food
Other	Any behavior not otherwise listed (e.g. allogrooming)

[a]Based on Stevenson and Poole, 1976.

nary cortisol concentrations. A two-factor, repeated-measures ANOVA was carried out to determine whether behavior changed over time following the stressor (on the day that the stressor was administered). The factors analyzed were stress and time period as well as the interaction between the two. Separate analyses were carried out initially for trained and nontrained animals.

After this, a three-factor mixed ANOVA was carried out using behavioral data from both groups of animals. This was to see if there was an effect of training on behavior and to increase the sample size effectively by combining both sets of data. The variables analyzed were stress, time period, and training.

Significance was set at $\alpha < 0.05$ throughout the analyses. Where significant main effects were found using repeated-measures ANOVAs, where appropriate, post-hoc pairwise t tests with the Bonferroni correction were used. These were intended to pinpoint in which differences lay, while controlling against Type II errors. For behavioral data, to ensure statistical independence, a single mean was calculated from both animals in a pair. Each pair, therefore, was effectively treated as one individual in the analysis. Data used consisted of mean sample points per session; 20 sample points were obtained per pair per 5 min session.

RESULTS

Behavioral Analyses

For trained animals, there was significantly less Inactive after the stressor compared with before it (see Table 2 and Figure 1). There also was an effect of time

TABLE 2
Results of Within-Subjects Analysis of Variances of Effects of Stressor, Time
of Observation and the Interaction Between the Two Variables on All Behaviors
for Trained Animals

	Stressor		Time		Stressor × Time	
Behavior	F(1, 5)	p	F(2, 10)	p	F(2, 10)	p
Inactive	36.14	< .01	3.05	.09	2.48	.13
Locomote	4.00	.10	4.37	< .05	1.79	.22
Self-Scratch	0.63	.47	2.25	.16	0.92	.43
Scent Mark	4.22	.10	1.34	.31	0.54	.60

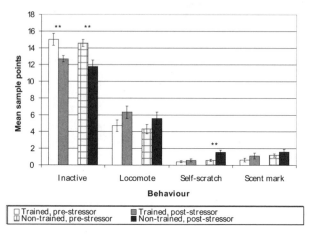

FIGURE 1   Mean sample points spent performing each behavior pre- and poststressor, for trained and nontrained animals (collapsed across 1200h, 1400h, and 1600h; bars represent standard errors).

of observation on Locomote (see Table 2). However, no significant differences between the individual observation times were found. There were no significant interactions between the variables of stressor and time for any of the behaviors (see Table 2).

For nontrained animals, there was significantly less Inactive behavior after the stressor compared with before it (see Figure 1). There was significantly more Self-Scratch behavior after the stressor compared with before it (see Figure 1). There was no effect of time of observation on behavior (see Table 3). The only behaviors that showed a significant interaction between time and stressor were Inactive and Self-Scratch (see Table 3; see Figures 2 and 3). Levels of Inactivity remained relatively stable over time for the prestressor condition; after the stressor, they were reduced dramatically at 1200h. At 1400h, poststressor levels had risen slightly. They

TABLE 3
Results of Within-Subjects Analysis of Variances of Effects of Stressor, Time of Observation and the Interaction Between the Two Variables on All Behaviors for Nontrained Animals

Behavior	Stressor		Time		Stressor × Time	
	$F(1, 5)$	p	$F(2, 10)$	p	$F(2, 10)$	p
Inactive	33.06	< .01	3.16	.09	4.72	< .05
Locomote	3.57	.12	0.62	.56	0.67	.53
Self-Scratch	25.97	< .01	1.16	.35	9.83	< .01
Scent Mark	2.30	.19	0.57	.58	0.78	.49

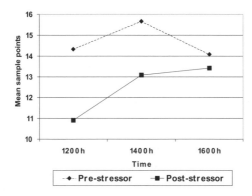

FIGURE 2   Interaction between stressor and time for Inactive (nontrained animals).

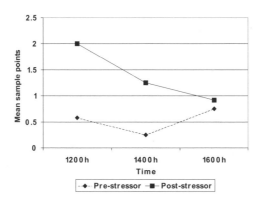

FIGURE 3   Interaction between stressor and time for Self-Scratch (nontrained animals).

227

rose again at 1600h, with rates similar pre- and poststressor at this time. The inverse of this was seen for self-scratch, with prestressor levels similar throughout all three time periods. However, after the stressor, levels were much higher at 1200h than for the prestressor period. The difference between pre- and poststressor data was reduced at 1400h and virtually was eliminated at 1600h.

When data for trained and nontrained animals were combined, there was significantly less Inactive behavior after the stressor compared with before it. There also was significantly more Locomote, Self-Scratch, Scent Mark after the stressor compared with before it (see Table 4; see Figure 4). Frequencies of Self-Scratch were significantly lower in trained than nontrained animals (see Table 4; see Figure 4). There were significant interactions between training and stressor for Self-Scratch (see Table 4; see Figure 5). Although there was a very slight increase in the amount of Self-Scratch seen in trained animals after the stressor, there was a

TABLE 4
Results of Within-Subjects Analyses of Variance of Effects of Stressor, Training, and the Interaction Between the Two Variables on All Behaviors

	Stressor		Training		Stressor × Training	
Behavior	F(1, 22)	p	F(1, 10)	p	F(1, 10)	p
Inactive	73.82	< .001	0.14	.72	< 0.01	.96
Locomote	7.08	< .05	0.98	.35	0.72	.42
Self-Scratch	14.47	< .01	5.17	< .05	6.61	< .05
Scent Mark	6.24	< .05	1.46	.25	0.05	.83

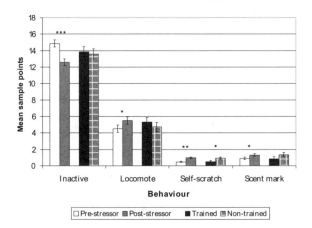

FIGURE 4 Mean sample points spent performing each behavior before and after the stressor (for trained and nontrained animals combined) and for trained and nontrained animals (before and after the stressor combined; collapsed across 1200h, 1400h, and 1600h; bars represent standard errors).

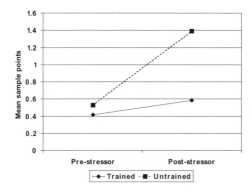

FIGURE 5   Interaction between the variables training and stress for Self-Scratch (collapsed across 1200h, 1400h, and 1600h).

large increase in the amount shown by nontrained animals. The prestressor levels of Self-Scratch were similar for both groups; whereas, after the stressor, nontrained animals scratched more than did the trained individuals.

Cortisol Analysis

When prestressor data were compared with data collected on the day of the stressor, there were no significant effects of time or stress on urinary cortisol, $F(2, 18) = 0.92$, $p = .42$, and $F(1, 9) = 4.45$, $p = .06$, respectively (see Figure 6).

DISCUSSION

There was a significant reduction in inactivity following administration of the stressor for both trained and nontrained animals. This behavior was the only one that the stressor affected significantly for the trained animals. Possibly, therefore, a decrease in the amount of time spent inactive may be the most sensitive measure of stress for this species.

There was no difference in the time trained animals spent locomoting pre- and poststressor. When data for the two groups were combined, however, there was a significant increase in locomotion poststressor. This is likely to be due to the increased sample size obtained by pooling data from the two groups. These results suggest that, in studies with at least a large sample size, increased levels of locomotion may be a useful and relatively long-lasting measure of stress and possibly reduced welfare. In support of this, Smith, McGreer-Whitworth, and French (1998) found locomotory behavior to be positively correlated with urinary cortisol in Weid's black, tufted-ear marmosets when housed alone in a novel cage.

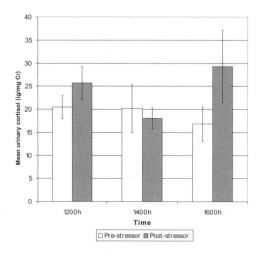

FIGURE 6   Mean concentrations of urinary cortisol at three prestressor time periods and the same three time periods on the day of administration of a stressor (stressor given between 0930h and 1030h; bars represent standard errors).

There was no significant difference in amount of self-scratching following the stressor in the trained animals. However, the nontrained animals showed a significant increase in self-scratching poststressor. When data for trained and nontrained animals were pooled, there also was an overall significant increase in self-scratching poststressor. The interaction between stress and time for the combined data of trained and nontrained animals indicated that the greatest increase in self-scratching occurred during the earliest observations following the stressor (i.e., at 1200h). Increases in self-scratching, in common with decreases in inactivity, persist for at least 4 hr following stressor administration and were observed at 1400h. Rates of both these behaviors, however, returned to almost prestressor levels by 1600h.

Self-scratching is thought to be a displacement activity in primates, which occurs during situations of tension, anxiety, frustration, conflict, and stress (Maestripieri, Schino, Aureli, & Troisi, 1992). In pharmacological studies, benzodiazepine anxiolytic drugs have been found to reduce the frequency of self-scratching in the common marmoset (Barros, Boere, Huston, & Tomaz, 2000; Cilia & Piper, 1997).

When pre- and poststressor values were combined, the amount of self-scratching was significantly higher in nontrained than trained animals. The positive interaction between training and stress showed that whereas trained animals showed no difference in scratching poststressor, there was an increase in self-scratching in the nontrained animals following the stressor. The fact that amount of self-scratching was similar for both groups prestressor suggests that training animals has no effect on their prestressor, undisturbed behavior. However, evidenced by the similarity between pre- and poststressor levels of self-scratching, being exposed to training procedures may mean that these animals are less affected by stressors than are their nontrained counterparts.

Some researchers consider scent marking to be an anxiety-related behavior in the marmoset, as it is affected by various classes of anxiolytic drugs (Cilia & Piper, 1997). In this study, frequency of scent marking was not significantly different in trained or nontrained animals following the stressor. When data from both groups were pooled, however, there was a significant increase in this behavior poststressor. This suggests that increases in scent marking may be an indicator of stress in this species, albeit less sensitive and requiring a larger sample size to show significance than, for example, self-scratching. There was no significant difference between trained and nontrained animals in the amount of scent marking observed, indicating that training was not a confounding variable on scent-marking behavior.

This study has resulted in a behavioral index of welfare for the common marmoset and has broad implications for the assessment and subsequent improvement of welfare in this species. The measures identified are simple, noninvasive, and easy to implement. They could be used by technicians to assess welfare implications of variations in scientific and husbandry procedures. It should be noted, however, that many behaviors may have wide ranges of acceptable time budgets within which welfare is not compromised. The challenge remains to be able to quantify what frequencies of each behavior are normal and acceptable and at what stage changes in behavioral frequency actually may represent a threat to welfare.

The marmosets in this study showed no significant differences in urinary cortisol levels in relation to the stressor. Possibly, a significant result may have been obtained with a larger sample size. Other studies have found clear increases in urinary cortisol in callitrichid primates in response to a stressor. Isolation in a small cage for approximately 11 hr produced significant increases in urinary cortisol in Weid's black tufted-ear marmosets (Smith & French, 1997).

The stressor used possibly may not have been aversive enough to provoke a physiological reaction in the trained animals in this study. Supporting this suggestion these animals (the only ones from which urine was collected) showed very little behavioral change following the stressor. Smith and French (1997) used isolation for 11 hr in a novel cage as a stressor; in this study, animals were removed from the homecage for approximately 4 min and, for part of that time, still were in contact with their pair mates. The presence of the familiar pair mate during part of, and following, the stressor also may have attenuated the behavioral and physiological response. The presence of familiar peers has been shown to reduce the impact of stressors in Weid's black tufted-ear marmosets (Smith et al., 1998). However, it should be noted that even the brief routine stressor used in this study in the presence of a familiar pair mate resulted in behavioral changes associated with stress for an extended period of time. Inactivity and self-scratching did not return to prestressor levels in the nontrained marmosets until 1600h, 6 hr after the stressor.

The increased human contact and interaction that the marmosets underwent because of the training for urine collection also may have had a beneficial effect on their reactions to being handled and temporarily removed from the homecage. Fear responses in the stressor situation may have been lessened due to the marmosets' previous experience with human interaction, which mainly was comprised of positive reinforcement and frequent rewards. The trained animals therefore may have perceived the stressor differently than did the nontrained animals, who had less prior experience of positive human interaction. Psychological factors play a significant role in the stress response (Mason, 1968); changed perception of the stressor, therefore, may have altered behavioral and physiological reactions to it. Common marmosets accustomed to handling and bi-weekly cage transfers did not show an immediate elevation in plasma cortisol when exposed to a novel environment with an unfamiliar, opposite-sex partner (Norcross & Newman, 1999). The results of this study, therefore, suggest that exposing marmosets to positive human interaction may help them to cope better with routine laboratory procedures such as being removed from the homecage and weighed.

ACKNOWLEDGMENTS

This research was funded by a studentship from the Biotechnology and Biological Sciences Research Council and a grant from the Faculty of Human Sciences, University of Stirling, for which we are grateful. We also would like to thank the staff at the MRC Unit for their help during the study, Universities Federation for Animal Welfare for providing funding that enabled the results to be presented at the 19th International Primatological Society Congress in China. We thank Mark Prescott and Nicki Cross for comments on the article.

REFERENCES

Barros, M., Boere, V., Huston, J. P., & Tomaz, C. (2000). Measuring fear and anxiety in the marmoset (*Callithrix penicillata*) with a novel predator confrontation model: Effects of diazepam. *Behavioral Brain Research, 108,* 205–211.
Bazer, F. W. (1998). *Endocrinology of pregnancy.* Totowa, NJ: Humana.
Cilia, J., & Piper, D. C. (1997). Marmoset conspecific confrontation: An ethologically-based model of anxiety. *Pharmacology, Biochemistry and Behavior, 58,* 85–91.
Crockett, C. M. (1998). Psychological well-being of captive nonhuman primates: Lessons from laboratory studies. In D. J. Shepherdson, J. D. Mellen, & M. Hutchins (Eds.), *Second nature: Environmental enrichment for captive animals* (pp. 129–152). Washington, DC: Smithsonian Institution Press.
Duncan, I. J. H., & Fraser, D. (1997). Understanding animal welfare. In M. C. Appleby & B. O. Hughes (Eds.), *Animal welfare* (pp. 19–31). Wallingford, England: CAB.
Grandin, T. (1997). Assessment of stress during handling and transport. *Journal of Animal Science, 75,* 249–257.
Hanson, J. D., Larson, M. E., & Snowdon, C. T. (1976). The effects of control over high intensity noise on plasma cortisol levels in rhesus monkeys. *Behavioral Biology, 16,* 333–340.

Hearn, J. P., Abbott, D. H., Chalmers, P. C., Hodges, J. K., & Lunn, S. F (1978). Use of the common marmoset *(Callithrix jacchus)* in reproductive research. *Primatological Medicine, 10*, 40–49.

Hennessy, M. B. (1997). Hypothalamic-pituitary-adrenal responses to brief social separation. *Neuroscience and Biobehavioral Reviews, 21*, 11–29.

Johnson, E. O., Kamilaris, T. C., Carter, C. S., Calogero, A. E., Gold, P. W., & Chrousos, G. P. (1996). The biobehavioral consequences of psychogenic stress in a small, social primate *(Callithrix jacchus jacchus)*. *Biological Psychiatry, 40*, 317–337.

Mason, G. J., & Mendl, M. (1993). Why is there no simple way of measuring animal welfare? *Animal Welfare, 2*, 301–319.

Mason, J. W. (1968). A review of psychoendocrine research on the pituitary-adrenal-cortical system. *Psychosomatic Medicine, 30*, 576–607.

McKinley, J., Buchanan-Smith, H. M., Bassett, L., & Morris K. (2003/this issue). *Training common marmosets* (Callithrix jacchus) to cooperate during routine laboratory procedures: Ease of training and time investment. *Journal of Applied Animal Welfare Science, 6*, 209–220.

Noldus Information Technology. (1993). The observer: System for collection and analysis of observational data [Computer software]. Wageningen, The Netherlands: Author.

Norcross, J. L., & Newman, J. D. (1999). Effects of separation and novelty on distress vocalizations and cortisol in the common marmoset *(Callithrix jacchus)*. *American Journal of Primatology, 47*, 209–222.

Reimers, T. J., Salerno, V. J., & Lamb, S. V. (1996). Validation and application of solid-phase chemiluminescent immunoassays for diagnosis of endocrine diseases in animals. *Comparative Haematology International, 6*, 170–175.

Reinhardt, V., Liss, C., & Stevens, C. (1995). Restraint methods of laboratory non-human primates: A critical review. *Animal Welfare, 4*, 221–238.

Smith, T. E., & French, J. A. (1997). Psychosocial stress and urinary cortisol excretion in marmoset monkeys *(Callithrix kuhli)*. *Physiology and Behavior, 62*, 225–232.

Smith, T. E., McGreer-Whitworth, B., & French, J. A. (1998). Close proximity of the heterosexual partner reduces the physiological and behavioral consequences of novel-cage housing in black tufted-ear marmosets *(Callithrix kuhli)*. *Hormones and Behavior, 34*, 211–222.

Stevenson, M. F., & Poole, T. B. (1976). An ethogram of the common marmoset *(Calithrix jacchus jacchus)*: General behavioral repertoire. *Animal Behavior, 24*, 428–451.

Tietz, N. W. (1976). *Fundamentals of clinical chemistry*. Philadelphia: Saunders.

Williams, J. B. (1987). *Behavior of captive marmosets and tamarins* (Callitrichidae*): A bibliography, 1975–1987*. Washington, DC: Primate Information Center.

JOURNAL OF APPLIED ANIMAL WELFARE SCIENCE, 6(3), 235–246
Copyright © 2003, Lawrence Erlbaum Associates, Inc.

Primate Training at Disney's Animal Kingdom

Hollie Colahan and Chris Breder

Disney's Animal Kingdom
Lake Buena Vista, Florida

A training program has been in place at Disney's Animal Kingdom since the nonhuman animals first arrived at the park. The Primate Team and the Behavioral Husbandry Team have worked together closely to establish a philosophy and framework for this program. This framework emphasizes setting goals, planning, implementing, documenting, and evaluating. The philosophy focuses on safety, staff training, and an integrated approach to training as an animal management tool. Behaviors to be trained include husbandry and veterinary as well as behaviors identified for specific species, individuals, or situations. Input from all the teams was used to prioritize these behaviors. Despite the challenges to maintaining such a program, the benefits to animal care and welfare have been enormous.

Since the first primates arrived at Disney's Animal Kingdom (DAK) in 1997, a training program has been in place to assist in providing them the best care possible. As the collection and the primate team have grown, so has the scope of the training program. The goals and philosophy, however, have remained the same. They will continue to guide the program into the future.

Two teams are responsible for primate training at DAK. Currently, the Primate Team is made up of 16 keepers who are involved in direct animal care such as daily husbandry, enrichment, and training; 3 zoological managers, who are responsible for overseeing the animal care and supervising and training the staff; and a curator of mammals who oversees the Primate Team in addition to other areas of the park. The Behavioral Husbandry Team, made up of two zoological managers, a part time curator, and a full time curator, provides leadership, support, staff training, and resources for the entire animal care team in animal training and enrichment (see Figure 1).

Requests for reprints should be sent to Hollie Colahan, Animal Programs, Disney's Animal Kingdom, P.O. Box 10000, Lake Buena Vista, FL 32830. E-mail: hollie.j.colahan@disney.com

The Primate Team animal collection contains 7.3 (7 males and 3 females) western lowland gorillas (*Gorilla gorilla gorilla*) housed as two groups of 4.0 and 3.3, 2.4 white cheeked gibbons (*Nomascus leucogenys*) housed as two groups of 1.2, 1.1 siamangs (*Hylobates syndactylus*); 3.6 mandrills (*Mandrillus sphinx*); 2.3 black and white colobus monkeys (*Colobus guereza*); and 1.1 mona monkeys (*Cercopithecus mona*). This is not an inclusive list of all the primates at DAK but is the extent of the collection discussed in this article.

PHILOSOPHY AND FRAMEWORK

The Behavioral Husbandry Team, in partnership with a cross section of Animal Care teams (area curators, zoological managers, and keepers), created a mutually agreed on list of expectations. This list became our philosophy of animal training at DAK (Mellen & Sevenich MacPhee, 2001):

1. Safety (animal, keeper, equipment, process, guest) is our first consideration in any training initiative.
2. All keepers and zoological managers must understand and articulate the animal training philosophy that was taught in a required Training Methods class. All keepers must be able to articulate and apply animal training techniques to achieve training goals as outlined by their team.

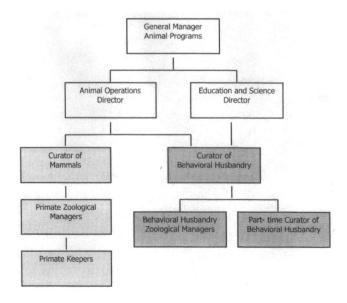

FIGURE 1   The reporting relationships of the Behavioral Husbandry Team and Primate Team at Disney's Animal Kingdom.

3. There is no separation between animal training and animal management. All keepers/zoological managers are trainers. All trainers are keepers/zoological managers.

4. Training is one of the many animal management tools that we use to facilitate good animal care. Many of the behaviors trained specifically facilitate medical care, often allowing us to avoid immobilizing or physically restraining an animal for treatment. We choose immobilization or restraint versus training based on the amount of time needed to train, the severity and urgency of the illness or injury, and the benefit to the animal. Sometimes it is not possible to use training techniques during a particular husbandry or medical procedure and various levels of restraint or immobilization are necessary.

5. A successful training program is proactive, not reactive. In other words, planning is an important part of a successful training program.

6. Keepers should routinely review past training records for patterns. For example, training records can be used to assess routine causes of periodic aggression, or identify differences in relative success in training various behaviors. Keepers can use these past records to predict situations that may be the precursors to breakdown in trained behaviors. Zoological managers periodically ask keepers if these reviews have been completed.

7. All keepers must learn about the natural and individual history of the animals for whom they care and train. When training, keepers need to assess and understand how the animal's natural and individual history affects that animal during the training process. Zoological managers make sure that keepers have, and use, this knowledge.

8. Keepers use a variety of methods to shape behavior. The focus of the training program at DAK is operant conditioning using positive reinforcement as the primary tool. Negative reinforcement (e.g., walking behind an animal to herd) and punishment (e.g., a time out—when the trainer stops the session because of noncooperation) also may be appropriate in some situations. It is mandatory for the trainers to fill out a training approval and planning form to communicate how they intend to train a particular behavior. Any method selected should make the most sense for that animal, based on the natural and individual history. The zoological manager makes sure that a form is completed and approved prior to the onset of training.

9. When training, keepers work together as a team. The goal is a completed behavior trained to the level that other members of the team also can have the animal perform it successfully. The success should be the animals and the team's, not just the person's who initially trained the behavior. The zoological managers facilitate the integrated approach.

In an effort to create a consistent animal training program among all animal care teams at DAK, a mutually agreed on process or framework was created

(Sevenich MacPhee, & Mellen, 1999). The framework is used by all animal care teams to develop, initiate, and maintain area training programs (www.animaltraining.org). The components of this framework are setting goals, planning, implementing, documenting, evaluating, and readjusting desired programmatic and behavioral goals. This framework is referred to as the S.P.I.D.E.R. (using the first letters of each of the framework components) model and is taught as part of an American Zoo and Aquarium Association (AZA) course, Managing Animal Enrichment and Training Programs (see Figure 2).

Setting Goals

The first component of the S.P.I.D.E.R. model is an opportunity to identify clearly the desired behaviors to be trained and how the natural and individual history of the animals may affect the training. The process of setting goals includes input from the Animal Care staff, veterinarians, park operations and entertainment, and horticulture staff.

Planning

The second component of the model specifically involves the development of a training plan, clearly outlining steps of how the behavior will be trained. Many times, the training may look very different from the plan that has been laid out. However, the exercise (i.e., creating a training plan) helps to fine tune what the trainers want to reinforce as well as what they do not want to reinforce. A formal or written training plan has many additional benefits, including the sharing of information with others and getting approval from the zoological managers.

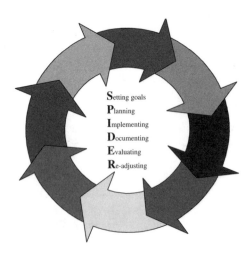

FIGURE 2   The S.P.I.D.E.R. Training Program Framework.

Implementing a Training Plan

This is simply the execution of the training plan and shaping the animal's behavior towards the desired goal.

Documenting

This is a critical part of the process for a variety of reasons, including the sharing of information about how the training sessions are progressing.

Evaluating

This allows the trainer to look back at trends over time.

Readjusting

Reviewing the training plan may indicate a readjustment.

Priority Behaviors

Behaviors to be trained are prioritized based on the goals of the animal care, veterinary, and research teams. Some of these goals are applied to the entire collection, and others pertain to specific species or individuals. As the animal care team prepared to open the park 5 years ago, shifting animals on and off exhibit was a priority behavior. Later, after this behavior was established, additional behaviors such as stationing, cooperative feeding, and separations became the training focus. The veterinary team also influenced priorities; behaviors were trained that facilitated the inspection of body parts for wound treatment and administration of medications. Specific behaviors for animals with medical conditions also were identified, such as a face presentation for a mandrill needing eye drops after cataract surgery. Finally, behaviors—urine collection and artificial insemination—that could help facilitate research projects were identified and prioritized (see Table 1).

Shift, Station, and Scale Training

Shifting was the first behavior the team focused on both for the guest experience and for animal management. For the holding areas to be cleaned during the day and for exhibit work to be done at night, animals consistently must shift in and out. It also is important to be able to shift animals off exhibit in the event of unexpected events such as retrieving an object dropped into the exhibit or other safety issues.

Additional husbandry behaviors that received early focus included stationing animals at specific locations or separating individual animals from the group so

TABLE 1
Behaviors Trained With Primates at Disney's Animal Kingdom

Behavior	Primary Purpose	Species
Back	Husbandry	All
Back of hand	Husbandry	All
Belly	Husbandry	All
Chest	Husbandry	All
Chin	Husbandry	All
Cooperative feeding	Husbandry	All
Ear	Husbandry	All
Face	Husbandry	All
Foot	Husbandry	All
Forearm	Husbandry	All
Hand	Husbandry	All
Head	Husbandry	All
Infant care	Husbandry	Gorilla, Gibbon, Mandrill
Knee	Husbandry	All
Open mouth	Husbandry	All
Scale	Husbandry	All
Separation	Husbandry	All
Shoulder	Husbandry	All
Side	Husbandry	All
Station	Husbandry	All
Tail	Husbandry	Colobus
Target	Husbandry	All
Thigh	Husbandry	All
Tongue	Husbandry	All
Ear thermometer	Veterinary	All
Injection	Veterinary	All
Oral medications	Veterinary	All
Stethoscope	Veterinary	All
Ultrasound	Veterinary	All
Wound cleaning: spray	Veterinary	All
Wound cleaning: swab	Veterinary	All
X-ray	Veterinary	Gorilla, Mandrill
Semen collection	Research	Gorilla, Mandrill
Urine collection	Research	Gorilla, Mandrill, Gibbon

that animals could be visually inspected and receive medications. Some animals proved difficult to separate but relatively easy to station, whereas others were quick to leave their station but separated readily. Depending on species and individuals, there are differences in behavior that can be trained first. Stationing and separating allow one keeper to train several animals alone. Individual animals, group dynamics, and availability of keeper staff are all factors when deciding which technique to use.

Scale training allows weights to be recorded routinely and, if needed, for animals to be monitored more closely. For larger species, a permanent floor scale is used. Smaller species use portable scales that can be removed from the enclosure after the training session. Crate training also is a priority for species needing to be moved regularly or who are scheduled for shipment to another institution. All primates coming into quarantine are crate trained to avoid an additional immobilization when moved to their permanent area when quarantine is complete.

Infant Care

Infant care training is a priority for animals who are first-time mothers or who have a history of poor maternal care. Infant assessment and supplementation are the primary goals, the ultimate goal being to keep the infants with their social groups. Training includes desensitizing the pregnant female to a variety of objects such as bottles and cooperative feeding as well as training the female to pick up an object and bring it to the front of the enclosure. The goal is to establish an infant care training program that will take into account the individual animal's particular deficiencies in maternal care (Philipp, Breder, & MacPhee, 2001; Richards, Owen, Mullins-Cordier, & Sellin, 2001).

There are six primary training goals for pregnant females:

1. Separation—to develop acceptance in case temporary removal from the group is required or a closer assessment of the infant is needed;
2. Pick up object—to develop the behavior of picking up her offspring if she should place the infant on the ground;
3. Pick up object and present the object at the mesh—to develop the behavior of allowing the animal care staff to get a close visual inspection of the infant to assess health status;
4. Pick up object and hold ventrally—to develop the behavior that encourages the female to place the infant in a proper nursing position;
5. Breast manipulation—to allow animal care staff to assess if the female is lactating and desensitize the breast to a nursing infant; and
6. Appropriate hold—to bridge and reward the female for holding the infant appropriately.

Soon after birth, a training program is begun for the infant to complement the female's training as well as to assist with the medical needs of the infant. Although the specific behaviors of this program require the infant's participation, it is critical that the female allow her infant to be interactive with animal care staff. In the case of an infant gibbon who had to be hand reared, this training allowed him to be reintroduced to the group much sooner because he was able to cooperate with the animal care staff consistently without requiring separation from the group.

There are six primary training goals for infants:

1. Station—once the infant is mobile, the infant comes to the front of the holding area where the trainer is to participate in the session;
2. Body part presentations—priorities depend on medical needs;
3. Separation—if needed, infant separates from the female for medical care;
4. Administration of oral medication—infant takes liquid from a syringe, such as oral polio vaccine or cold medicine;
5. Bottle feeding—feeding occurs without infant's being removed from the female; and
6. Injections—infant positions body part for injections, such as pediatric vaccine series.

Training for Veterinary Care

The Primate zoological managers and the Behavioral Husbandry Team meet with the veterinarians to discuss priority medical behaviors to be trained. These include behaviors that will facilitate immobilizations such as injection or an "open mouth" behavior for an oral anesthetic agent. Both of these behaviors also are useful in administering medications. In many cases, additional training can help avoid immobilizations. Presentation of body parts and desensitization to medical instruments and treatments often allow the veterinarian to assess the animal without immobilizing. Integrating of the Veterinary Team into the training program is an important factor in successfully training medical behaviors. Although this requires an additional time commitment from them, the veterinarians and technicians can assess the animals better when the animals no longer react to them negatively; the Animal Care Team benefits from the feedback the Veterinary Team can provide on things like injection techniques (Siever, Walsh, Weber, & MacPhee, 2001).

Individual animals or species with specific medical concerns may require additional priority behaviors (Colahan, Mangold, & Philipp, 2001). Ultrasound training is a priority for pregnant animals of any species as well as for individuals with other medical conditions. Animals requiring regular medication receive additional focus on injection or open mouth behaviors. Unforeseen injuries also may create new training priorities, such as two gorillas and a mandrill with injured hands who were trained to position for a portable X-ray machine, avoiding additional immobilizations through anesthesia.

Training of Specific Behaviors

Both internal and external research projects may prompt additional training of specific behaviors. Urine collection is the most common request for research projects, used for monitoring reproductive cycles, measuring cortisol levels, and monitoring pregnancy. Animals are trained to station at the front of the holding area in the morning and urinate on cue where the keepers can collect it.

The need to find a balance between maintaining a genetically healthy population also housed in natural social groups has prompted the Gorilla Species Survival Plan to investigate sex selection through artificial insemination. If animals can be trained for semen collection and insemination, the need for immobilizations and, therefore, the associated health risk, is reduced. This project also includes the need for urine collection to measure hormone levels and hormone injections for ovulation ("Gorilla Husbandry Training," 2002).

TIME INVESTMENT

The initial time investment to establish an integrated, sustainable animal training program, train the staff, and train naïve animals can seem overwhelming, but the long-term advantages quickly become apparent. A few extra minutes each day over a few weeks training an animal to shift can avoid hours of baiting, pushing, and pleading with an animal to come inside every night. Although some keepers may be reluctant at first, most are eager to learn and use these skills both to make their day more efficient and provide better care of the animals. However, because these techniques were not used widely in zoos until relatively recently, not all keepers have acquired the skill set. All keepers at DAK attend a two-part class and then pair with an experienced mentor because the rest is best learned in the field.

Consistency is the key to successful training. It works best when all the keepers use the same technique every day when training a new behavior. This requires managers to provide the training and support to the entire staff and ensure that the agreed on training plans are being implemented. Initially, this requires additional time for both staff and animal training, and the buy-in at all levels is critical for success. Once the program is established, the maintenance of established behaviors and progress on new ones can be achieved in a few minutes each day.

CHALLENGES

At DAK, we have a large number of people caring for the animals in the collection. Because of this, one of our greatest challenges is consistency. The gorilla building houses 10 gorillas, and three to four keepers work the area each day. This means that no fewer than five people work the area in any given week. Consistency in the area always is the top priority when creating this schedule; vacations, call-ins, and turnover only add to this number. Although having a large staff has been beneficial to many aspects of our training program, it also creates our greatest challenge.

To address this challenge, we adhere to guidelines. When an animal is learning a new behavior, only the primary trainer for that animal trains the behavior. This makes the training as consistent as possible during the most critical time and allows the animal to build a relationship and trust with one keeper at a time. Other keepers can ask for any behaviors that have already been trained with that animal. This allows all keepers to participate in training all the animals, and training can continue when the primary trainer is not present.

For group behaviors such as shifting and separations, we have found that using one trainer for the entire group is the most successful method. Early on, we felt that it was important to make the inside holding area a positive, appealing place to be. Although shifting animals inside rarely is a problem, getting them to go outside can be a challenge. Even though the outdoor exhibits are complex, enriching places where the animals are fed their favorite food items, the indoor holding areas are familiar, climate controlled, and where keeper interactions take place. Today, the shifting behavior is solid. Occasionally, however, the behavior begins to break down and the team always goes back to one keeper who trains it consistently until it becomes solid again.

Separations is another behavior we have trained this way. Although some species have had no problem with this behavior, our gorillas were challenging. After attempting several different methods, success came when one keeper trained the entire group. In the past, separations often had been associated with immobilizations, and this contributed to the challenges surrounding this behavior. Regular training sessions include one trainer per animal; up to six trainers plus observers are in the holding area for a session. When doors started closing, the animals became anxious and began leaving their stations and trying to block the doors. With one trainer in the hallway, the atmosphere is quiet. This makes it easier for the animals to keep track of what doors are closing and to maintain eye contact with the trainer throughout the behavior, increasing their comfort level and the trainer's success.

The use of designated primary trainers allows keepers to build relationships with the animals they train, and this trust can lead to faster progress when training new behaviors. However, these feelings of ownership can make it difficult for individuals to let go and allow someone else to train that animal when the situation calls for it. We have developed a program where our success has come from using different methods depending on the situation.

BENEFITS

The benefits to our training program have been both obvious and subtle. The differences in immobilizations and the need for other veterinary treatment are apparent.

Instead of animals being immobilized for minor injuries, they can be assessed and treated because of being trained to perform the behaviors necessary for treatment. Thus, the number of immobilizations is reduced. When immobilizations are necessary, they begin with the animal voluntarily separating and accepting a hand injection for anesthesia instead of fleeing from dart guns. This has made these procedures easier and safer for the keepers, veterinarians, and animals.

The more subtle benefits are seen in the day-to-day management. Animals shift in and out reliably and present body parts for inspection. Animals are weighed regularly, urine is collected for analysis, and medications are administered more easily. When special circumstances arise, requiring specific training, such as research projects or medical needs, the foundations are already in place to achieve these behaviors more quickly and easily.

CONCLUSIONS

By following a framework and establishing a consistent, self-sustaining training program, we have created an environment that better addresses the needs of both the animals and the staff and that will continue to evolve as the institution grows. Although the program certainly requires a time investment and faces occasional challenges, the benefits have been enormous. Training, as an integral part of day-to-day management at DAK, has become an indispensable tool in providing uncompromising animal care.

ACKNOWLEDGMENTS

We thank Marty MacPhee and Jill Mellen for their support of the primate training program at DAK and their assistance with this article, and Nancy Hawkes and the entire Primate Team at DAK for their tireless work caring for the animals in our collection and their assistance with this article.

REFERENCES

Colahan, H., Mangold, B., & Philipp, C. (2001, May). Matters of the heart: Managing cardiomyopathy in a male gorilla. In *The apes: Challenges for the 21st century conference Proceedings, 2000* (p. 366). Brookfield, IL: Chicago Zoological Society.

Gorilla husbandry training for assisted reproduction at Disney's Animal Kingdom. (2002). [Videotape]. Lake Buena Vista, FL: Disney's Animal Kingdom. [Available from Hollie Colahan, Disney's Animal Kingdom, P.O. Box 10000, Lake Buena Vista, FL 32830]

Mellen, J., & Sevenich MacPhee, M. (2001). Philosophy or environmental enrichment: Past, present, and future. *Zoo Biology, 20,* 211–226.

Philipp, C., Breder, C., & MacPhee, M. (2001, May). Maternal care and infant training of a western low-land gorilla (*Gorilla gorilla gorilla*). In *The apes: Challenges for the 21st century conference Proceedings, 2000* (pp. 135–136). Brookfield, IL: Chicago Zoological Society.

Richards, B., Owen, L., Mullins-Cordier, S., & Sellin, R. (2001, May). The lesser known ape: Husbandry training with gibbons and siamangs. In *The apes: Challenges for the 21st century conference Proceedings, 2000* (pp. 107–111). Brookfield, IL: Chicago Zoological Society.

Sevenich MacPhee, M., & Mellen, J. (1999, May). *Framework for successful training and enrichment.* Paper presented at the Pan African Association of Zoos, Aquariums, Botanical Gardens, Cape Town, South Africa.

Siever, D., Walsh, P., Weber, B., & MacPhee, M. (2001, May). Operant conditioning of apes to facilitate medical procedures and immobilizations. In *The apes: Challenges for the 21st century conference Proceedings, 2000* (pp. 137–139). Brookfield, IL: Chicago Zoological Society.

JOURNAL OF APPLIED ANIMAL WELFARE SCIENCE, 6(3), 247–261
Copyright © 2003, Lawrence Erlbaum Associates, Inc.

The Development of an Operant Conditioning Training Program for New World Primates at the Bronx Zoo

Gina Savastano, Amy Hanson, and Colleen McCann

Mammal Department
Bronx Zoo/Wildlife Conservation Society
Bronx, New York

This article describes the development of an operant conditioning training program for 17 species of New World primates at the Bronx Zoo. To apply less invasive techniques to husbandry protocols, the study introduced behaviors—hand feeding, syringe feeding, targeting, scale and crate training, and transponder reading—for formal training to 86 callitrichids and small-bodied cebids housed in 26 social groups. Individual responses to training varied greatly, but general patterns were noted among species. With the exception of lion tamarins, tamarins responded more rapidly than marmosets, Bolivian gray titi monkeys, and pale-headed saki monkeys in approaching trainers and learning behaviors. Marmosets, in comparison to most tamarins, had longer attention spans. This meant that fewer, lengthier sessions were productive whereas shorter, more frequent sessions were most successful for tamarins. Among the cebids, pale-headed saki monkeys needed relatively few sessions to perform basic and advanced behaviors whereas Bolivian gray titi monkeys were less responsive and progressed at a deliberate pace. Marked changes in the animals' behavior during daily husbandry procedures, their voluntary participation in training activities, and the disappearance of aggressive threats toward care staff indicated that training reduced stress and improved the welfare of the animals. During daily training displays, zoo visitors experienced interactive animals while learning the importance of low-stress animal husbandry.

Despite their abundance in captive collections, to date relatively few operant conditioning training programs involving callitrichid primates (marmosets, tamarins, and Goeldi's monkeys) have been developed. This may be due partly to their flighty nature and small physical stature (Epple, 1975; McKinley, Buchanan-Smith, Basset,

Requests for reprints should be sent to Gina Savastano, Mammal Department, Bronx Zoo, Wildlife Conservation Society, 2300 Southern Boulevard, Bronx, New York 10460. E-mail: gsavastano@ wcs.org

& Morris, 2003/this issue; Mittermeier, Rylands, Coimbra-Filho, & Fonesca, 1988; Rylands, 1993). Traditional methods of transporting or monitoring health status in the callitrichids often required physical restraint, with concomitant stress, resulting in animals becoming fearful or aggressive toward their caretakers (Brownie & McCann, 2003; Farmerie, Neffer, & Vacco, 1999). In studies investigating indicators of stress in marmosets, a significant increase in locomotor (Smith, McGreer-Whitworth, & French, 1998) and scent-marking behaviors (Barros, Mello, Huston, & Tomaz, 2001) was found when animals were presented with a negative stimulus. Additionally, in a comparative study of trained and untrained marmosets, Bassett, Buchanan-Smith, McKinley, and Smith (2003/this issue) demonstrated that stress imposed by invasive husbandry procedures was mitigated by exposure to operant conditioning training, illustrating the positive benefits of applying operant conditioning training to captive husbandry techniques.

The ability to detect signs of illness, weight loss, and pregnancy, as well as monitoring injuries, medicating and transporting individuals is essential for the appropriate care and management of captive collections. The ability to conduct necessary husbandry procedures in a low stress manner while building a positive rapport with each individual should be a primary goal for all captive primate caretakers (Colahan & Breder, 2003/this issue; Laule & Desmond, 1995; Reichard, Shellabarger, & Laule, 1992).

The Bronx Zoo's (BZ) New World primate collection includes 86 callitrichids and small-bodied cebids, totaling 17 species, housed in three separate facilities. The primary objective for developing a formal operant conditioning program for the BZ's New World primates was to decrease the level of stress involved in typical husbandry routines, and consequently, improve the welfare of the animals in our collection. In addition to advancing basic husbandry protocols, positive reinforcement training has the added benefit of providing a stimulating, enriching, and trusting environment for the animals (Laule, 1992). This in turn enhances the zoo visitor experience by exhibiting animals who are engaged in their environment, spend less time retreating to nestboxes and other hidden spaces, and can be viewed actively participating in training sessions (Laule & Desmond, 1998).

In this article, we describe the development of a formal training program for a large and diverse New World primate collection involving various care staff, making note of important elements that formed the foundation of the program and the results of the first year of the program.

METHODS

Study Animals and Housing Conditions

Eighty-six individual animals of 17 species of New World primates participated in the first year of the training program (see Table 1). Animals are housed in so-

TABLE 1
Participating Study Animals Within the Training Program

Group	Species[a]	Common Name	Group Composition		Group Classification
			No. of Males	No. of Females	
1	*Callithrix jacchus*	Common marmoset	1	4	Family
	Pithecia pithecia	Pale-headed saki monkey	1	1	Breeding
2	*Callithrix kuhlii*	Wied's tufted-eared marmoset	0	2	Single-sex female
	Callicebus donacophilus	Bolivian gray titi monkey	2	3	Family
3	*Callithrix kuhlii*	Wied's tufted-eared marmoset	0	2	Single-sex female
4	*Callithrix argentata*	Silvery marmoset	2	1	Family
5	*Callithrix argentata*	Silvery marmoset	1	2	Family
6	*Callithrix argentata*	Silvery marmoset	3	3	Family
7	*Callithrix pygmaea*	Pygmy marmoset	2	0	Single-sex male
8	*Callithrix geoffroyi*	Geoffroy's tufted-eared marmoset	0	2	Single-sex male
9	*Callithrix geoffroyi*	Geoffroy's tufted-eared marmoset	1	3	Family
10	*Saguinus mystax*	Mustached tamarin	1	2	Single-sex female
11	*Saguinus oedipus*	Cotton-top tamarin	1	4	Family
12	*Saguinus bicolor*	Pied tamarin	1	1	Breeding
13	*Saguinus geoffroyi*	Geoffroy's tamarin	3	3	Family
14	*Saguinus geoffroyi*	Geoffroy's tamarin	2	1	Family
15	*Saguinus geoffroyi*	Geoffroy's tamarin	1	1	Breeding
16	*Saguinus midas*	Golden-handed tamarin	0	3	Single-sex female
17	*Saguinus midas*	Golden-handed tamarin	1	1	Breeding
18	*Saguinus midas*	Golden-handed tamarin	1	1	Breeding
19	*Saguinus imperator*	Emperor tamarin	2	0	Single-sex male
	Callicebus donacophilus	Bolivian gray titi monkey	2	1	Family
20	*Leontopithecus chrysopygus*	Black lion tamarin	1	1	Breeding
21	*Leontopithecus rosalia*	Golden lion tamarin	2	3	Family
22	*Leontopithecus rosalia*	Golden lion tamarin	2	0	Single-sex male
23	*Leontopithecus chrysomelas*	Golden-headed lion tamarin	2	0	Single-sex male
24	*Callimico goeldii*	Goeldi's monkey	1	1	Breeding
25	*Pithecia pithecia*	Pale-headed saki monkey	1	1	Breeding
26	*Pithecia pithecia*	Pale-headed saki monkey	1	1	Breeding

Note. Two species listed under the same group number indicate a mixed-species group.

[a]Taxonomy follows Groves (1993).

cial groups, which we classify as either a breeding pair (one male and one female), family group (breeding pair with one or more offspring), or single-sex group. In some cases, the primates are housed in mixed-species groups.

Animals in the training program are housed in indoor glass-fronted naturalistic exhibits. These exhibits are viewable to the public from 1000h to 1600h daily. Enclosures vary in size but are approximately 2 m wide × 1.5 m deep × 3 m high. Exhibit furnishings include natural branches, natural and artificial vines, a nestbox, plastic plants, and a pine-bark mulch substrate over a concrete floor. Exhibit floors, glass, and plants are spot-cleaned daily; the mulch substrate is removed and the enclosures disinfected weekly. Most animals have access to an off-exhibit enclosure overnight, measuring approximately 1.5 m wide × 1 m deep × 3 m high. These enclosures are furnished with natural branches and enrichment items (puzzle feeders, foraging boxes, and gum-arabic feeders) and are cleaned daily. The animals are fed twice daily, in the morning between 0830h and 1000h and in the afternoon between 1400h and 1600h. Training sessions are conducted in the animals' exhibit spaces during public viewing hours. Frequently, there are visitors observing the sessions.

Materials

Equipment utilized in the training program is listed in Table 2. The training crates have mesh sides and two plexiglass guillotine doors: one on one end and one side of the crate (see Figure 1). When in the crate, the animals receive their food rewards through the mesh sides of the crate. Some crates are configured with clips so that two crates can be attached along side each other with the side doors lined up to each other. This set-up works well for larger groups as animals that come into the crate can be locked into one side, leaving the other side open for additional animals to enter.

Because of the callitrichids' small physical size, food rewards and amounts used in the training program were determined by consultation with the zoo's nutritionist. The most commonly used rewards include small pieces of banana or grape, apple sauce, gum arabic, crickets, waxworms, and mealworms with amounts equaling 10% of the caloric value of the total diet. Food given during training sessions is removed from the animal's daily diet to avoid over feeding and skewing the recommended diet.

Behaviors

The behaviors that the animals are trained to do, and their defining criteria, are listed in Table 3. Basic behaviors identified to be most important for animal management include hand feeding, syringe feeding, targeting, scale and crate

TABLE 2
Equipment Used in Training Program

Item	Use
Clicker (Click and Treat™)	Bridge
Wooden dowel—1 cm diameter × 20 cm long	Target
Quick-draw Training Pouch™	To hold food rewards
1 cc plastic syringes	To dispense food rewards
Beaded pony-tail holders of different colors	Stations
Small plastic battery-operated scale, platform size 14cm × 14cm (Ohaus model LS200™)	To obtain weights on callitrichids
Large metal battery-operated scale, platform size 30cm × 40cm (Weigh-tronix model QC3265™)	To obtain weights on callitrichids, titi and saki monkeys
Wooden crates with two plexiglass doors and mesh sides (30cm × 30cm × 40cm)	For crate training callitrichids
Wooden crates with two plexiglass doors and mesh sides (40cm × 40cm × 50cm)	For crate training titi and saki monkeys
Aluminum platforms 40cm × 50cm, 1m high	For setting the large scale and training crates on
Plexiglass platform 14cm × 19cm, 1m high	For setting the small plastic scale on
Transponder reader (Avid Power Tracker IV™)	To detect identifying transponder microchips in animals

FIGURE 1   Crate training with a family group of cotton-top tamarins (*Saguinus oedipus*). Note the two crate set-up that is advantageous for training with larger groups (see text). (Photo credit: Julie Larsen/Wildlife Conservation Society)

TABLE 3
Behaviors Trained in the Training Program

Behaviors	Verbal Cue	Visual Cue	Criteria
Basic behaviors			
Hand feed	—	Food in hand	Animal takes the treat either in their hand or mouth directly from the trainer's hand
Syringe feed	—	Presence of syringe	Animal takes liquid from a syringe
Target	Target	Point to target or extend target to animal	Animal touches nose to the tip of the target and holds until released by bridge
Station	Station	Point to ponytail holder	Animal sits within one body length of their specific colored ponytail holder
Scale	Scale	Point to scale	Animal sits on the scale and stays until released by bridge
Crate	Box	Point to crate	Animal enters crate and waits while door is closed
Transponder read	—	Transponder reader	Animal stands on all fours while transponder wand is passed along their back and shoulder blades
Advanced behaviors			
Up	Up	Index finger pointed up	Animal stands up on legs and holds until released by bridge
Palpate	Belly	Index finger pointed up	Animal stands up on legs and holds while trainer manipulates their hand along the animal's abdomen
Back	Back	Keeper holds own hand above animal's back	Animal sits while trainer runs his/her hand down the length of the animal's back
Tail	Tail	Keeper holds own hand above animal's tail	Animal sits while trainer runs his/her hand down the length of the animal's tail
Hand	Hand	Keeper holds own index finger sideways in front of animal	Animal places the appropriate hand on trainer's finger (appropriate hand is determined by which side of the body the trainer's finger is on)
Stethoscope	—	Presence of stethoscope	Animal sits while stethoscope is placed on their chest, abdomen, and back
Otoscope	Ear	Presence of otoscope	Animal sits while an otoscope is placed in their ear
Ultrasound	Up/belly	Presence of ultrasound equipment	Animal holds in an Up position on a t bar while their abdomen is prepped with gel and an ultrasound wand placed and moved around on their abdomen

Note. An em dash (—) = no verbal cue used.

training, and transponder reading. After a group has learned to perform all of the basic behaviors, advanced behaviors that include tactile manipulations are introduced (see Table 3). Behaviors are trained through positive reinforcement; the animals receive rewards for performing desired behaviors, whereas undesired behaviors are ignored. Standard operant conditioning techniques using clickers as bridges and successive approximations are used (Laule, Bloomsmith, & Schapiro, 2003/this issue; Pryor, 1999).

Program Organization

Six keepers form the core group of trainers in the program. Each trainer is scheduled to work a minimum of 3 days each week with the New World primate collection. Trainers are allotted two 30-min training sessions per day. Within each session, approximately 5 min is spent on preparation, 10 min on training, 5 min on equipment removal and clean-up, and 10 min on record keeping.

Each trainer serves as the primary trainer for two or three groups of monkeys. Primary trainers are responsible for introducing new behaviors to the animals (see Figure 2). Once a behavior is consistently performed by an animal according to established criteria, other keepers act as secondary trainers. The secondary trainers assist in maintaining established behaviors and are available to work with the animals in the primary trainer's absence. Each team member involved serves as a primary trainer on some groups as well as a secondary trainer on others. Daily records

FIGURE 2   A Geoffroy's tamarin (*Saguinus geoffroyi*) takes a food treat from a syringe while being palpated. (Photo credit: Julie Larsen/Wildlife Conservation Society)

are kept and bi-monthly meetings are held to track training progress and to facilitate communication among the trainers and animal department managers.

RESULTS

The training program is ongoing and continues to develop as both the staff and animals advance their skills. Here we present the results from the first year of the program.

Logistical Challenges

Initiating and maintaining a training program for New World primates at the BZ posed several challenges due to the size of the primate collection, the unavoidable rotation of keeper staff throughout the various animal facilities, and the movement of animals between facilities for exhibit and husbandry purposes. Maintaining training consistency between keepers and animals required significant attention. To address this, uniform training criteria were created, written records of training sets were kept, and weekly meetings were held for communication.

Animal Challenges

In addition to logistical challenges, animal challenges were, and always will be, encountered. Table 4 lists some of the animal challenges that we encountered and the techniques used to overcome them.

The trainers observed that the animals' responses to training varied greatly among individuals, groups, and species (see Table 5). The results show a wide range in the number of sessions conducted prior to a behavior being successfully accomplished by most of the animals in the groups as well as differences among species in which behaviors were learned successfully. Hand feeding from a keeper took from 1 to 150 training sessions, syringe feeding from 1 to 10 sessions, targeting from 1 to 8 sessions, entering a crate from 1 to 20 sessions, going onto a scale from 1 to 75 sessions, going to a color-coded station from 1 to 40 sessions, and allowing their implanted microchip identification transponders to be read from 1 to 3 sessions. Ten of the groups responded particularly well to training and were taught advanced behaviors (see Table 6).

DISCUSSION

Although training session length varies between species, the data in Tables 5 and 6 are useful in providing an indication of species differences in the time in-

TABLE 4
Animal Challenges Within the Training Program

Challenge	Solution
Food rewards: avoiding obesity	Consult with the staff nutritionist to establish approved reward items and quantities
Identifying animals and their motivations for training	Maintain records describing physical characteristics of individuals and their reward preferences
Training large groups	Establish control by training individuals to station
Timid individuals	Use a single trainer to develop a trust bond, introduce bolder, or previously trained animals to the group
Overeager, dominant, or aggressive individuals	Ask overeager animals to station at a distance so that the trainer can focus on others; also, offer a time-consuming reward such as nuts with shells, super mealworms, or whole grapes that keep the overeager animal occupied

vestment required for training of basic and advanced behaviors. Although some animals participated in the training program immediately and performed all of the basic behaviors within five training sessions (e.g., Group 6, silvery marmosets), others required months even to accept hand feeding (e.g., Group 21, golden lion tamarins).

Tamarins

In general, lion tamarins were relatively slow to become comfortable with training. Building a rapport with each individual animal was a lengthy process, and relatively long training sessions were needed. On the contrary, tamarins (*Saguinus spp.*) responded more quickly than all marmosets and cebids with regard to approaching trainers as well as learning behaviors. Individuals would become engaged immediately as the trainer entered the enclosure and set up materials, volunteering to begin the training session. However, *Saguinus spp.* lost interest in sessions more rapidly than did marmosets or cebids. Shorter, more frequent sessions throughout the day proved most productive for *Saguinus spp.* Pied tamarins stopped responding to the trainer after just a few minutes into the sessions. However, if the trainer left the enclosure and then re-entered a short time (even < 1 min) later, they generally regained interest. Thus, a schedule that provided up to 10 short training sets a day was the most productive for this species.

Marmosets

In general, marmosets took longer than tamarins or cebids to begin interacting with the trainer. However, once a bond was formed and a behavior established,

TABLE 5
Time Scale for Training Basic Behaviors

Group	Species[a]	Hand Feed	Syringe Feed	Target	Station	Scale	Crate	Transponder Read
						No. of Training Sessions for Animals to Perform Behavior			
1	*Callithrix jacchus*	60	2	1	40	1	1	1
	Pithecia pithecia	1	b	c	c	2	10	0
2	*Callithrix kuhlii*	20	5	4	c	3	7	2
	Callicebus donacophilus	30	c	c	c	2[d]	10	c
3	*Callithrix kuhlii*	10	5	5	8	3	5	1
4	*Callithrix argentata*	1	1	2	b	1	3	c
5	*Callithrix argentata*	2	1	6	c	1[d]	2	3
6	*Callithrix argentata*	1	2	2	5	2	4	1
7	*Callithrix pygmaea*	90	c	c	c	2[d]	4	c
8	*Callithrix geoffroyi*	1	3	1	c	1	6	1
9	*Callithrix geoffroyi*	2	2	b	b	2	2	c
10	*Saguinus mystax*	5	2	1	c	1	5	c
11	*Saguinus oedipus*	5	3	c	c	10	10	c
12	*Saguinus bicolor*	1	1	8	c	1	1	1
13	*Saguinus geoffroyi*	4	1	1	c	1	1	1
14	*Saguinus geoffroyi*	1	10	1	c	7	8	c
15	*Saguinus geoffroyi*	20	b	b	c	9	c	c
16	*Saguinus midas*	2	1	c	c	4	4	c
17	*Saguinus midas*	1	1	1	2	1	1	1
18	*Saguinus midas*	1	2	1	c	1	1	1
19	*Saguinus imperator*	1	1	2	2	3	5	1
	Callicebus donacophilus	20	c	c	c	3[d]	b	c
20	*Leontopithecus chrysopygus*	120	1	1	15	2	20	1
21	*Leontopithecus rosalia*	150	3	b	b	25	10	c
22	*Leontopithecus rosalia*	60	b	b	c	3[d]	b	c
23	*Leontopithecus chrysomelas*	15	c	c	c	3[d]	c	c
24	*Callimico goeldii*	50	b	b	b	75[d]	c	c
25	*Pithecia pithecia*	1	b	4	c	2	8	1
26	*Pithecia pithecia*	1	c	2	15	1	4	c

Note. This table indicates the number of training sessions it took for most of the animals in the groups to perform the behaviors.

[a]See Table 1 for the common names. [b]Behavior is being trained. [c]Training for this behavior has not been started. [d]Behavior is done while trainer is outside enclosure.

TABLE 6
Time Scale for Training Advanced Behaviors

		No. of Training Sessions for Animals to Perform Behavior							
Group	Species[a]	Up	Palpate	Back	Tail	Hand	Stethoscope	Otoscope	Ultrasound
1	Callithrix jacchus	2	6	2	8	10	1	12	20
	Pithecia pithecia	10	[b]	[b]	8	10	20	[b]	[b]
4	Callithrix argentata	2	[b]	[b]	2	[b]	b	[b]	[b]
6	Callithrix argentata	2	[b]	b	b	b	b	[b]	[b]
9	Callithrix geoffroyi	2	[c]	[b]	2	[b]	b	[b]	[b]
16	Saguinus midas	3	7	5	2	[b]	6	[b]	[b]
17	Saguinus midas	2	4	3	1	[b]	5	[b]	[b]
19	Saguinus imperator	2	2	5	1	[b]	2	2	[b]
20	Leontopithecus chrysopygus	3	[b]	b	[b]	5	[b]	[b]	[b]
25	Pithecia pithecia	8	[b]	b	[b]	15	[b]	[b]	[b]
26	Pithecia pithecia	2	[b]	[b]	2	10	[b]	[b]	[b]

Note. This table indicates the number of training sessions it took for most of the animals in the groups to perform the behaviors.
[a]Common names are given in Table 1. [b]This behavior has not yet been trained. [c]This behavior is being trained.

additional training progressed rapidly (see also, McKinley et al., 2003/this issue). Common marmosets took 60 sessions to hand feed, but several subsequent behaviors were learned in under 10 sessions. They are now one of the most advanced groups in our collection. Overall, marmosets responded best to few (one or two) longer sessions (10 to 15 min) throughout the day.

Pygmy marmosets were the most difficult of all the marmosets in the training program due to their shy nature and cautious disposition. Initially, the trainer had to be in the enclosure, unmoving, for 25 min before the animals would respond positively. Pygmy marmosets have slow, deliberate movements, and hand-feeding efforts were most successful when the trainer reached his or her hand out all the way to the animals and offered food rewards directly in front of their mouths—maintaining the greatest possible distance between trainer and animal. For all other species in the program, trainers held the food reward at various distances in front of the animals, so that they would approach and actively take the food item.

Pale-Headed Saki Monkeys

Among the cebids, pale-headed saki monkeys were the most enthusiastic training participants. As with the tamarin species, they immediately approached the trainer when he/she entered their enclosure and learned basic behaviors in relatively few sessions. Although saki monkeys learned rapidly, sessions often were interrupted or forced to end due to over-riding social interactions (the male was more interested in soliciting the female, diverting attention from training activities).

Bolivian Gray Titi Monkeys

Bolivian gray titi monkeys were the most difficult of all the species in the program to train. All individuals in the three groups were extremely shy and initially impossible to hand feed. With the introduction of less timid species from the training program (emperor tamarins and Wied's tufted-eared marmosets) to their exhibits, the titi monkeys began to approach trainers and hand feed. The introduction of more approachable individuals allowed titi monkeys to learn by observation. They also appeared to respond to competition with the other species for food rewards. Currently, all the titi monkeys hand feed and, on the condition that the trainer is outside their enclosure, stand on a scale, and enter a crate. To date, cooperative feeding of titi monkeys and either tamarins or marmosets in the same enclosure has been unsuccessful. The titi monkeys are still slow to approach the trainer, allowing the callitrichids to dominate the sessions. By separating the callitrichids into the overnight enclosure area (and rewarding them for doing so), the titi monkeys are able to participate in the training sessions.

Overall Positive Effects

Although quantitative data on indicators of stress were not collected, several changes in the animals' behavior indicate that the training program has substantially reduced the stress levels of the animals during specific husbandry procedures (crating and transporting animals) and has had an overall positive effect on the collection. Prior to the training program, the animals typically responded to the presence of keepers in their enclosures by moving to the highest area, retreating into nestboxes (and, with lion tamarins, closing the nestbox door), alarm calling, and/or displaying aggressive threats. After participation in the training program, they no longer threaten keepers when they enter the enclosure and, instead, eagerly approach and interact with the keepers and voluntarily participate in the training sessions. Thus, the rapport between the keeper staff and this collection has greatly improved, and the welfare of the animals has been enhanced. The observed behavioral changes in the trained animals are consistent with other studies reporting the positive effects of operant conditioning training on the psychological well-being of animals (Colahan & Breder, 2003/this issue; Farmerie et al., 1999; Laule & Desmond, 1995, 1998).

CONCLUSIONS

The New World primate operant conditioning training program at the BZ has bene-fited the public, keepers, and, most important, the animals in the program. The train-ing program has improved the visitor experience on two levels. Members of the pub-lic now view interactive animals engaged in their environment. They are more visible in their exhibits than they were prior to the establishment of the program and more frequently perch in the front of their enclosures where visitors can easily view them. The public also learns about the importance of enhancing the care of the ani-mals by applying low-stress husbandry techniques during our daily public displays and informational graphics describing the program.

For the animal keeper staff, working closely with the animals in the training program has been a very enriching and rewarding experience. Keepers are pro-vided an opportunity to know the animals on a more individual basis, interact with them in a positive way, and appreciate the benefits that the training has for the wel-fare of the animals in their care.

Finally, and most important, the training program benefits the animal collec-tion. The animals appear to be more comfortable during daily husbandry proce-dures, and their voluntary participation in the training program indicates that training is, on balance, a positive activity for them. Assessing the health and re-productive status of the animals through weight monitoring and tactile manipu-lations has substantially increased our ability to detect pregnancies, weight loss, obesity, and illness at early stages. The introduction of syringe feeding has facil-itated medicating individuals in a group and reduced the need to separate ani-mals from their group (to ensure medication consumption). Crate training has substantially reduced the need to capture and physically restrain animals, an ob-viously stressful procedure (Reinhardt, 2003/this issue), while simplifying the transport of animals among the various enclosures—a necessary activity for the exhibition of a zoo collection.

In conclusion, despite the various challenges involved in the development of a formal training program for a large, diverse primate collection, success can be at-tained if the goals of the program are prioritized and the available resources maxi-mized. More important, if enhancing the welfare of the animals remains the primary objective of the program, then the challenges encountered become the stimulus for new solutions.

ACKNOWLEDGMENTS

The Bronx Zoo New World primate training program would not be possible without the exemplary care and efforts of the training staff, Adele Barone, Nichole Morabito, Brian Putman, Nicole Rella, Nancy Rogers, and Kitty Dolan.

We thank the Mammal Department staff for their facilitation of the program, and Kevin Walsh for his assistance in our training efforts.

REFERENCES

Barros, M., Mello E. L., Huston, J. P., & Tomaz, C. (2001). Behavioral effects of buspirone in the marmoset employing a predator confrontation test of fear and anxiety. *Pharmacology Biochemistry and Behavior, 68*, 255–262.

Bassett, L., Buchanan-Smith, H. M., McKinley, J., & Smith, T. E. (2003/this issue). *Effects of training on stress-related behavior of the common marmoset* (Callithrix jacchus) in relation to coping with routine husbandry procedures. *Journal of Applied Animal Welfare Science, 6*, 221–233.

Brownie, A., & McCann, C. (2003, May). *Proceedings of the WCS Callitrichid Training and Enrichment Workshop.* New York: Wildlife Conservation Society.

Colahan, H., & Breder, C. (2003/this issue). Primate training at Disney's Animal Kingdom. *Journal of Applied Animal Welfare Science, 6*, 235–246.

Epple, G. (1975). The behavior of marmoset monkeys (*Callithricidae*). In L. A. Rosenblum (Ed.), *Primate behavior: Developments in field and laboratory research* (Vol. 4, pp. 195–239). New York: Academic.

Farmerie, M., Neffer, D., & Vacco, K. (1999). Enrichment and operant conditioning of callitrichids. In V. Sodaro & N. Saunders (Eds.), *Callitrichid husbandry manual* (pp. 64–89). Chicago: Chicago Zoological Park.

Groves, C. P. (1993). Order primates. In D. E. Wilson & D. M. Reader (Eds.), *Mammalian species of the world: A taxonomic and geographic reference* (2nd ed., pp. 243–277). Washington, DC: Smithsonian Institution Press.

Laule, G. (1992). Addressing psychological well-being: Training as enrichment. In *Proceedings of the American Association of Zoological Parks and Aquariums* (pp. 415–422). Wheeling, WV: American Association of Zoological Parks and Aquariums.

Laule, G. E., Bloomsmith, M. A., & Schapiro, S. J. (2003/this issue). The use of positive reinforcement training techniques to enhance the care, management, and welfare of laboratory primates. *Journal of Applied Animal Welfare Science, 6*, 163–173.

Laule, G., & Desmond, T. (1995). Use of positive reinforcement techniques to enhance animal care, research, and well-being. In K. A. L. Bayne & M. D. Kreger (Eds.), *Wildlife mammals as research models: In the laboratory and field. Proceedings of the American Veterinary Medical Association* (pp. 53–59). Bethesda, MD: Scientists Center for Animal Welfare.

Laule, G., & Desmond, T. (1998). Positive reinforcement training as an enrichment strategy. In D. J. Shepardsen, J. D. Mellen, & M. Hutchins (Eds.), *Second nature: Environmental enrichment for captive animals* (pp. 302–313). Washington, DC: Smithsonian Institution Press.

McKinley, J., Buchanan-Smith, H. M., Bassett, L., & Morris K. (2003/this issue). Training common marmosets (*Callithrix jacchus*) to cooperate during routine laboratory procedures: Ease of training and time investment. *Journal of Applied Animal Welfare Science, 6*, 209–220.

Mittermeier, R. A., Rylands, A. B., Coimbra-Filho, A., & Fonseca, G. A. B. (Eds.). (1988). *Ecology and behavior of neotropical primates* (Vol. 2). Washington, DC: World Wildlife Fund.

Pryor, K. (1999). *Don't shoot the dog: The new art of teaching and training* (Rev. ed.) New York: Bantam.

Reichard, T., Shellabarger, W., & Laule, G. (1992). Training for husbandry and medical purposes. In *American Association of Zoological Parks and Aquariums, Annual Conference Proceedings* (pp. 396–402). Wheeling, WV: American Association of Zoological Parks and Aquariums.

Reinhardt, V. (2003/this issue). Working with rather than against macaques during blood collection. *Journal of Applied Animal Welfare Science, 6,* 189–197.

Rylands, A. B. (Ed.). (1993). *Marmosets and tamarins: Systematics, behaviour and ecology.* Oxford, England: Oxford University Press.

Smith, T. E., McGreer-Whitworth, B., & French, J. A. (1998). Close proximity of the heterosexual partner reduces the physiological and behavioral consequences of novel-cage housing in black tufted-ear marmosets (*Callithrix kuhli*). *Hormones and Behavior, 34,* 211–222.

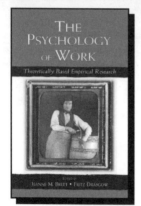

THE PSYCHOLOGY OF WORK
Theoretically Based Empirical Research
Edited by
Jeanne M. Brett
Northwestern University
Fritz Drasgow
University of Illinois at Urbana-Champaign
A Volume in LEA's Organization and Management Series
Series Editors: *Arthur P. Brief, James P. Walsh*
Associate Editors: *P. Christopher Earley, Sara L. Rynes*

This edited volume is derived from a conference held in honor of Charles Hulin's contribution to the psychology of work. His research has carefully developed and tested theory related to job satisfaction, withdrawal from work, and sexual harassment. Edited by Hulin's students, *The Psychology of Work* discusses research in job satisfaction. This research shows that job satisfaction plays an essential role in theories of organizational behavior. Formal models are used, such as item response theory, structural equation modeling, and computational models.

Three general and consistent themes in Hulin's research are represented in this book's chapters. The first theme is a focus on broad, general constructs, such as job satisfaction. The virtue of this approach is that a wide range of behavior can be explained by a small number of variables. The second theme involves the examination of the antecedents and consequences of job satisfaction. This theme is increasingly important because it ties research on job attitudes and job behaviors where links are consistently found and to social attitudes and behaviors where links are rarely found. The third theme consists of Hulin's interest in the use of formal models to characterize and understand behavior.

This volume will be of interest to scholars and students in industrial/organizational psychology, human resources, organizational behavior, and management.

Contents: A.P. Brief, J.P. Walsh, Foreword. J.M. Brett, F. Drasgow, Introduction. Part I: *The Hulin Legacy.* C.L. Hulin, Lessons From Industrial and Organizational Psychology. T.A. Judge, Back to the Same Place, for the First Time? The Hulin Family Tree. Part II: *Research on the Psychology of Work.* Section A: *Conceptualization of Psychological Constructs.* T.A. Judge, J.E. Bono, A. Erez, E.A. Locke, C.J. Thoresen, The Scientific Merit of Valid Measures of General Concepts: Personality Research and Core Self-Evaluations. H.M. Weiss, D.R. Ilgen, The Ubiquity of Evaluation: A Hulinesque Essay. H.C. Triandis, Motivation to Work in Cross-Cultural Perspective. Section B: *Antecedents and Outcomes of Satisfaction.* W.L. Richman-Hirsch, T.M. Glomb, Are Men Affected by the Sexual Harassment of Women? Effects of Ambient Sexual Harassment on Men. T.M. Probst, The Impact of Job Insecurity on Employee Work Attitudes, Job Adaptation, and Organizational Withdrawal Behaviors. P. Hom, The Legacy of Charles Hulin's Work on Turnover Thinking and Research. C.J. Sablynski, T.W. Lee, T.R. Mitchell, J.P. Burton, B.C. Holtom, Turnover: An Integration of Lee and Mitchell's Unfolding Model and Job Embeddedness Construct With Hulin's Withdrawal Construct. H.E. Miller, J.G. Rosse, Emotional Reserve and Adaptation to Job Dissatisfaction. Section C: *Modeling Organizational Behavior.* T.M. Glomb, A.G. Miner, Exploring Patterns of Aggressive Behaviors in Organizations: Assessing Model-Data Fit. R.A. Levin, M.J. Zickar, Investigating Self-Presentation, Lies, and Bullshit: Understanding Faking and Its Effects on Selection Decisions Using Theory, Field Research, and Simulation. S.T. Seitz, A.G. Miner, Models of Organizational Withdrawal: Information and Complexity.
0-8058-3815-5 [cloth] / 2002 / 352pp. / $69.95
Special Discount Price! $34.50
Applies if payment accompanies order or for course adoption orders of 5 or more copies.
No further discounts apply.
Prices are subject to change without notice.

Lawrence Erlbaum Associates, Inc.
10 Industrial Ave., Mahwah, NJ 07430–2262
201–258–2200; 1–800–926–6579; fax 201–760–3735
orders@erlbaum.com; www.erlbaum.com

2004 SUBSCRIPTION ORDER FORM

Please ❑ enter ❑ renew my subscription to:

JOURNAL OF APPLIED ANIMAL WELFARE SCIENCE

Volume 7, 2004, Quarterly — ISSN 1088–8705/Online ISSN 1532–7604

SUBSCRIPTION PRICES PER VOLUME:

Category:	Access Type:	Price: US-Canada/All Other Countries
❑ Individual	Online & Print	$50.00/$80.00

Subscriptions are entered on a calendar-year basis only and must be paid in advance in U.S. currency—check, credit card, or money order. Prices for subscriptions include postage and handling. **Journal prices expire 12/31/04. NOTE:** Institutions must pay institutional rates. Individual subscription orders are welcome if prepaid by credit card or personal check. **Please note:** A $20.00 penalty will be charged against customers providing checks that must be returned for payment. This assessment will be made only in instances when problems in collecting funds are directly attributable to customer error.

❑ **Check Enclosed** (U.S. Currency Only)   **Total Amount Enclosed $_____**

❑ **Charge My**: ❑ VISA ❑ MasterCard ❑ AMEX ❑ Discover

Card Number _____   Exp. Date_____/_____

Signature_____
(*Credit card orders cannot be processed without your signature.*)
PRINT CLEARLY for proper delivery. STREET ADDRESS/SUITE/ROOM # REQUIRED FOR DELIVERY.

Name_____

Address_____

City/State/ Zip+4_____

Daytime Phone #_____E-mail address_____
Prices are subject to change without notice.

For information about online subscriptions, visit our website at *www.erlbaum.com*

Mail orders to: **Lawrence Erlbaum Associates, Inc.,** Journal Subscription Department
10 Industrial Avenue, Mahwah, NJ 07430; **(201) 258–2200; FAX (201) 760–3735; journals@erlbaum.com**

LIBRARY RECOMMENDATION FORM

Detach and forward to your librarian.

❑ I have reviewed the description of the *Journal of Applied Animal Welfare Science* and would like to recommend it for acquisition.

JOURNAL OF APPLIED ANIMAL WELFARE SCIENCE

Volume 7, 2004, Quarterly — ISSN 1088–8705/Online ISSN 1532–7604

Category:	Access Type:	Price: US-Canada/All Other Countries
❑ Institutional	Online & Print	$320.00/$350.00
❑ Institutional	Online Only	$270.00/$270.00
❑ Institutional	Print Only	$290.00/$320.00

Name_____Title_____

Institution/Department_____

Address _____

E-mail Address_____
Librarians, please send your orders directly to LEA or contact from your subscription agent.
Lawrence Erlbaum Associates, Inc., Journal Subscription Department
10 Industrial Avenue, Mahwah, NJ 07430; **(201) 258–2200; FAX (201) 760–3735; journals@erlbaum.com**

FOR 2003 PRICES OR TO SUBSCRIBE TO VOLUME 6, 2003
PLEASE CONTACT JOURNAL CUSTOMER SERVICE AT **1-800-926-6579.**
2003 RATES EXPIRE 12/31/2003.

LEADERSHIP DEVELOPMENT

Paths to Self-Insight and Professional Growth

Manuel London
State University of New York at Stony Brook
A Volume in the Applied Psychology Series
Series Editors: Edwin A. Fleishman, Jeanette N. Cleveland

Leadership Development explores how leaders gain and use self-knowledge for continuous improvement and career development and describes how leaders help themselves and the people with whom they work, understand themselves, and become more self-determined, continuous learners, and make the most of resources, such as feedback and coaching. This book explains why leaders need support for self-insight and professional growth in today's business environment. It explores dimensions of effective leadership in light of business, technological, and economic trends. Focusing on the importance of leaders developing accurate self-understanding, the book defines self-insight, outlines the meaning of internal strength and resilience for self-regulation, and considers how leaders attain a meaningful and realistic sense of self-identity.

Leadership Development illustrates ways organizations support these psychological processes. Leadership development is viewed as a comprehensive, continuous process that includes evaluating organizational needs and individual competencies, setting goals for career development and performance improvement, offering needed training and growth experiences, providing feedback, and tracking change in behavior and performance over time. It describes how leaders react to feedback and how 360-degree feedback survey methods and executive coaching help leaders attain and apply self-insight to enhance their performance. In addition, this book considers challenges and opportunities for leadership development, including how leaders overcome career barriers and become continuous learners.

Contents: E.A. Fleishman, Series Foreword. Preface. Introduction: Dimensions of Effective Leadership. **Part I:** *Psychological Processes Underlying Leadership Behavior.* Self-Insight: Prerequisite for Understanding Others and the Environment. Self-Regulation: Processes for Maintaining Motivation and Resilience. Self-Identity: Personal Directions for Development. **Part II:** *Support for Leadership Development.* The Leadership Development Process. Feedback Processes. 360-Degree Feedback. Coaching Processes. Development Programs. **Part III:** *Challenges and Opportunities.* Overcoming Career Barriers. Becoming a Continuous Learner. Conclusion: Becoming a Principled, Diplomatic Leader.
0-8058-3851-1 [cloth] / 2002 / 304pp. / $79.95
0-8058-3852-X [paper] / 2002 / 304pp. / $34.50
Prices are subject to change without notice.

Order with confidence at www.erlbaum.com*!*
(WITH SECURE ONLINE ORDERING)

Lawrence Erlbaum Associates, Inc.
10 Industrial Ave., Mahwah, NJ 07430–2262
201–258–2200; 1–800–926–6579; fax 201–760–3735
orders@erlbaum.com; www.erlbaum.com

JOB FEEDBACK

Giving, Seeking, and Using Feedback for
Performance Improvement, Second Edition

Manuel London
State University of New York at Stony Brook
A Volume in LEA's Applied Psychology Series
Series Editor
Edwin A. Fleishman, Jeanette N. Cleveland

This book demonstrates how managers can be more effective in gathering and processing performance information about subordinates, making ratings on performance appraisals and multisource feedback surveys, and feeding back this information in a way that is nonthreatening and leads to productive changes in behavior. It also shows how employees can gather, accept, and use meaningful performance information from appraisals, surveys, and informal discussions to change their own behavior. In doing so, the volume suggests how human resource practitioners and training professionals can help managers give and use feedback more effectively.

Five years have elapsed since the first edition of *Job Feedback* was published. This revision covers the following updates in the field:
+ New theory and research on organizational performance management;
+ New methods for linking strategic planning with individual goal setting and development;
+ The emergence of globalization and cross-cultural factors affecting performance evaluations and the use of technology to collect performance data; and
+ New chapters on person perception, multisource feedback, team feedback, and feedback in multicultural organizations.

Contents: E.A. Fleishman, J.N. Cleveland, Series Foreword. Preface. Introduction. **Part I:** *Person Perception.* How and Why Feedback Works. How People Evaluate Themselves. Feedback Dynamics. Processing Information About Others. **Part II:** *Performance Evaluation Methods.* Performance Appraisals. Multisource Feedback Methods. The Usefulness of Multisource Feedback. Assessment Centers and Business Simulations. **Part III:** *Supporting the Use of Feedback.* The Manager's Role as Feedback Provider. Performance Management, Development, and Coaching. Holding Managers Accountable for Giving and Using Feedback. **Part IV:** *Future Directions.* Feedback in Teams and Cross-Cultural Organizations. Changing Technologies and Jobs: Toward Feedback-Oriented, Continuous Learning Environments.
0-8058-4494-5 [cloth] / 2003 / 280pp. / $59.95
0-8058-4495-3 [paper] / 2003 / 280pp. / $29.95
Prices are subject to change without notice.

Order with confidence at www.erlbaum.com*!*
(WITH SECURE ONLINE ORDERING)

Lawrence Erlbaum Associates, Inc.
10 Industrial Ave., Mahwah, NJ 07430–2262
201–258–2200; 1–800–926–6579; fax 201–760–3735
orders@erlbaum.com; www.erlbaum.com

MISBEHAVIOR IN ORGANIZATIONS

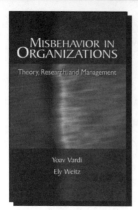

Theory, Research, and Management
Yoav Vardi
Ely Weitz
Tel Aviv University
A Volume in LEA's Applied Psychology Series
Series Editor
Edwin A. Fleishman, Jeanette N. Cleveland

For many years, scholars aligned with mainstream research paradigms that make up organizational behavior (OB) have been leaning toward the more positive depiction of organizational reality. To better understand people's behavior in the workplace, they must also explore misbehavior. Organizational Misbehavior (OMB) is a term that was coined by Yaov Vardi about 10 years ago when he found out there were no models for how to predict "misconduct" at work. Thus, the purpose of this book is to delineate a new agenda for organizational behavior theory and research.

Devoted to the study and management of misbehavior in work organizations, this volume is divided into three parts. Part I discusses the prevalence of these phenomena. It searches for typologies and definitions for misbehavior in the management literature using a historical perspective and proposes a general framework of OMB. Part II explores some important manifestations and antecedents of OMB at different levels of analysis—the person, the job, and the organization. Finally, Part III presents practical and methodological implications for managers and researchers. The authors offer a comprehensive and systematically developed framework for the development and management of misbehavior in organizations. The book is intended for students, scholars, and practitioners who manage OB.

0-8058-4332-9 [cloth] / 2004 / 360pp. / $79.95
0-8058-4333-7 [paper] / 2004 / 360pp. / $34.50
Prices are subject to change without notice.

Lawrence Erlbaum Associates, Inc.
10 Industrial Ave., Mahwah, NJ 07430–2262
201–258–2200; 1–800–926–6579; fax 201–760–3735
orders@erlbaum.com; www.erlbaum.com